WIND-PLOWED FURROWS IN CAPE COD SAND DUNES

TREES PRUNED BY SALT SPRAY ON FIRE ISLAND

SAND-KILLED TREES AT HERRING COVE, CAPE COD

CORDGRASS-LINED TIDAL CREEK IN A VIRGINIA SALT MARSH

WINTER SUNSET AT AMAGANSETT, LONG ISLAND

HURRICANE WAVES OFF CAPE HATTERAS

LIFE WORLD LIBRARY
LIFE NATURE LIBRARY
TIME READING PROGRAM
THE LIFE HISTORY OF THE UNITED STATES
LIFE SCIENCE LIBRARY
GREAT AGES OF MAN
TIME-LIFE LIBRARY OF ART
TIME-LIFE LIBRARY OF AMERICA
FOODS OF THE WORLD
THIS FABULOUS CENTURY
LIFE LIBRARY OF PHOTOGRAPHY
THE TIME-LIFE ENCYCLOPEDIA OF GARDENING
THE AMERICAN WILDERNESS
FAMILY LIBRARY
THE TIME-LIFE BOOK OF FAMILY FINANCE
THE TIME-LIFE FAMILY LEGAL GUIDE

ATLANTIC BEACHES

THE AMERICAN WILDERNESS/TIME-LIFE BOOKS/NEW YORK

BY JONATHAN NORTON LEONARD
AND THE EDITORS OF TIME-LIFE BOOKS

Published simultaneously in Canada.
Library of Congress catalogue card number 72-79775.

THE AMERICAN WILDERNESS
SERIES EDITOR: Charles Osborne
Editorial Staff for *Atlantic Beaches:*
Text Editor: L. Robert Tschirky
Picture Editor: Iris Friedlander
Designer: Charles Mikolaycak
Staff Writer: Gerald Simons
Chief Researcher: Martha T. Goolrick
Researchers: Joan Chambers, Margo Dryden, Villette Harris, Michael Luftman, Mollie E. C. Webster
Design Assistant: Mervyn Clay

Editorial Production
Production Editor: Douglas B. Graham
Quality Director: Robert L. Young
Assistant: James J. Cox
Copy Staff: Rosalind Stubenberg, Eleanore W. Karsten, Florence Keith
Picture Department: Dolores A. Littles, Joan Lynch

Valuable assistance was given by the following departments and individuals of Time Inc.: Editorial Production, Norman Airey, Nicholas Costino Jr.; Library, Peter Draz; Picture Collection, Doris O'Neil; Photographic Laboratory, George Karas; TIME-LIFE News Service, Murray J. Gart.

The Author: Jonathan Norton Leonard was brought up in Sandwich on Cape Cod and has studied the beach near his home there in all seasons. Science editor of TIME for 20 years, Leonard is now a freelance writer. His books include *Planets* in the LIFE Science Library and *Early Japan* and *Ancient America* in the TIME-LIFE BOOKS Great Ages of Man series.

The Cover: An incoming wave froths as it runs up the beach near Highland Light on Cape Cod.

Contents

A Wilderness Shared by Land and Sea

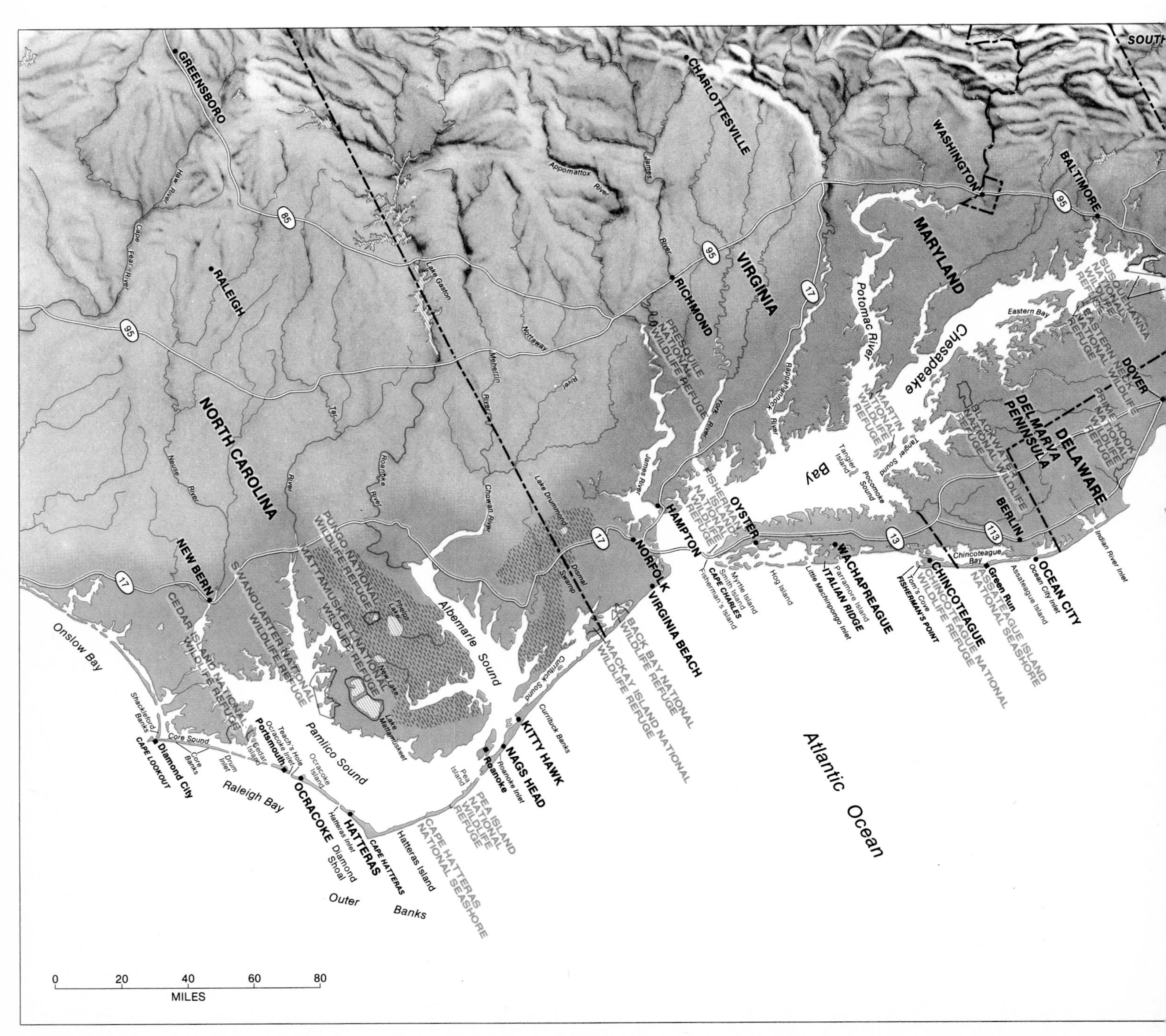

The coastal regions discussed in this book lie within the green rectangle at right and are highlighted in green on the detailed relief map below. This seaside wilderness, ranging between Cape Lookout in North Carolina and the coast north of Cape Cod in Massachusetts, includes 29 federally protected tracts of land with a total area of about 250,000 acres; these are outlined in red and labeled with red type. Rivers appear in blue, and marshes and swamps are designated by blue dashes. Points of special interest, such as Montauk Light at the eastern end of Long Island, are marked with black squares. Otherwise, standard map symbols are used: black dots for towns, double black lines for roads, crossbarred lines for railroads.

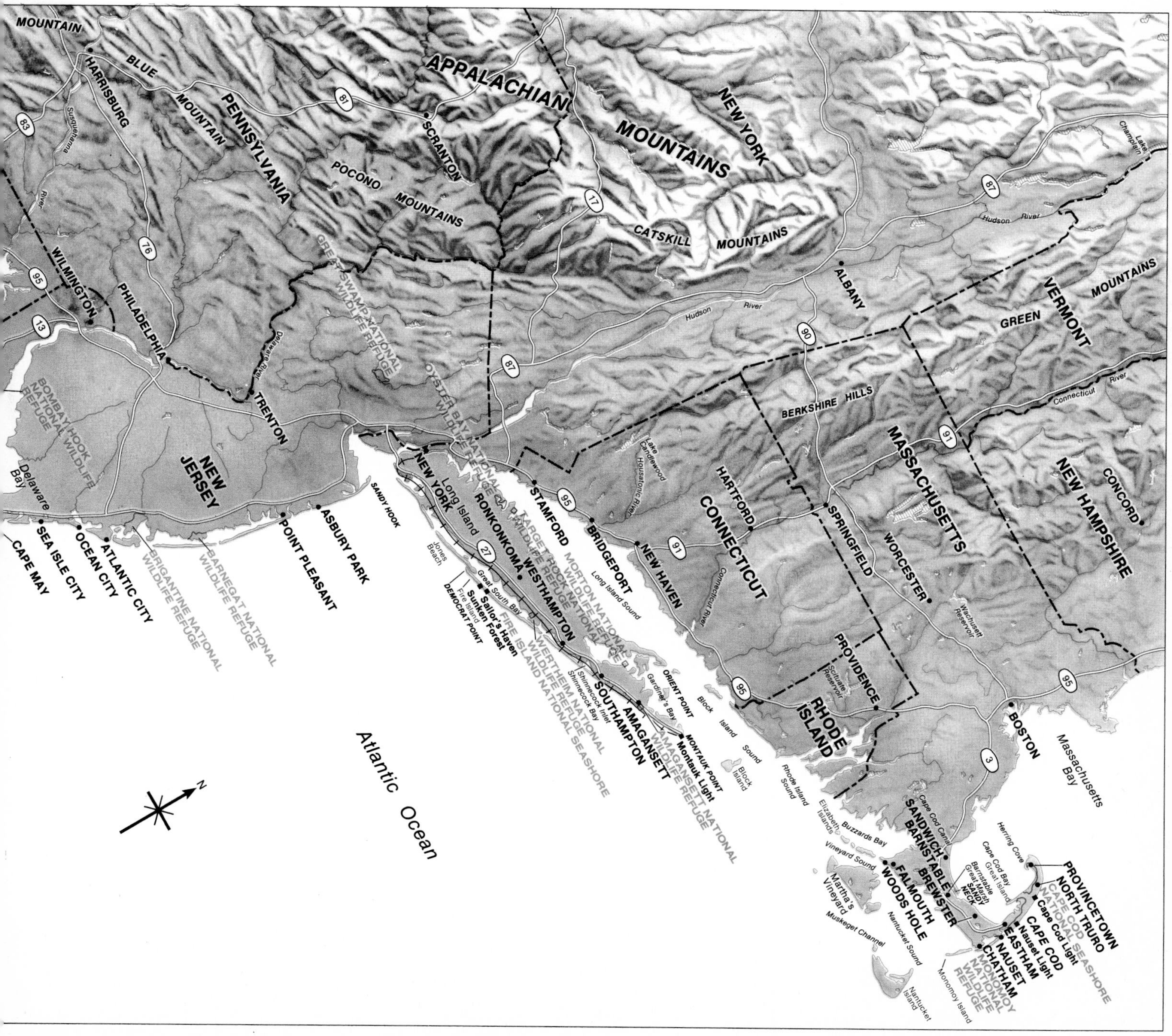

1/ Wind, Water and Sand

There is naked Nature—inhumanly sincere, wasting no thought on man, nibbling at the cliffy shore where gulls wheel amid the spray. HENRY DAVID THOREAU/ *CAPE COD*

My parents' home, when I was a small boy, was half a mile from a beach on Cape Cod. In the still of night—and the nights were stiller then—I lay awake to listen to the surf. Sometimes it boomed, and sometimes it roared, and I wondered why. Sometimes I heard the clang of the bell buoy off the mouth of the Cape Cod Canal, but often even when the wind blew hard and raised plenty of waves to swing its four great clappers, it was silent. Again I wondered why. And when the fog swept in from the sea and the long wail of the foghorn filled the night, I listened for its echoes. Sometimes I heard a train of them diminishing slowly to silence. Sometimes I heard none. I still do not know why.

When I was a bit older I was permitted to walk on the town beach. I felt the sand shake when a great wave fell on it. I watched the little petrels (Mother Carey's chickens, we called them) flying fast and low and dipping their delicate bills into the leaping water. When a great storm blew, all sorts of people walked on the beach: old ladies swaddled in multiple sweaters and whipping raincoats, children fighting against the wind, grown men in sou'westers taking time off from work to stand, legs braced apart, smiling at the surf. Cape Codders are friends of the sea. They wish it well and cheer its attacks on the land. To them it means the ultimate wilderness that will never be tamed by men.

It means that to me and, as I have found to my pleasure, to a great many people born far inland. Some of them insist that one must be on a seagoing ship or at least some kind of boat to appreciate the power and majesty of the ocean. I have done a lot of sailing, and I disagree. A beach is far better. Here is the battleground between the ocean and the land. Here is the surf, which varies from gentle and playful to awesomely violent. Here the tides move forward and back, stranding the shells of clams and sand dollars and horseshoe crabs. Here is a rich assembly of easily visible life, the fascinating and beautiful creatures, from the darkness-loving ghost crab to the voracious herring gull, that has learned to survive on the battlefield.

Since my shoreside childhood I have explored and admired hundreds of beaches, and I have learned that they vary a good deal. They have different sand, different water, waves and wind, different smells, different dunes and marshes behind them, different living things in the water, land and air. Some of the differences are subtle and some spectacular. I have seen the beaches of black-lava sand in Hawaii, the white-coral sand of the Bahamas, the stony beaches of the French Riviera where near-naked vacationers lie packed on the rocks like Pribilof seals. The strangest beach of all was a small semicircular one on the Dutch West Indian island of Curaçao. On a fence hung a warning sign in Dutch: *Pas op diep water* (Watch out for deep water). The beach had no sand at all, only what appeared to be broken human leg bones. They were bulb-ended shafts of coral, probably washed in from a reef offshore. Across the mouth of that macabre cove was stretched a steel shark net meant to protect swimmers. But it had a hole in it, and a great gray shark was swimming fiercely around trying to get out. So I did not attempt to swim at the Beach of Broken Bones.

This book will not attempt to describe all the beaches I have seen; it will deal only with those I know on our own Atlantic coast from Cape Cod in Massachusetts to Cape Lookout in North Carolina. North of Cape Cod the coast is increasingly rock-bound, and most of the beaches are narrow, like webs of skin between stony fingers of the land. South of Cape Lookout the beaches are usually wide and flat, with very fine, firmly packed sand and with waves breaking far out. Some of these beaches lie on the seaward side of large, low islands that are the common delta of several big rivers washing down from the upland. Behind them are narrow inlets and wide salt marshes that gradually change to fresh-water swamps. This is alligator and water-moccasin country, palmetto country, the country of great gnarled live oaks with gray beards of Spanish moss swaying from their limbs. It is a foreign coast to me, and I leave it for others to describe.

The straight-line distance from Provincetown on the tip of Cape Cod to Cape Lookout is 625 miles. The actual length of the shoreline would be hard to measure because some of it includes river and creek banks, but it is many times—perhaps 10 times—longer. By no means all of this coastal strip is wilderness. On Long Island, for instance, the coast is only relatively untouched, and long stretches of the New Jersey shore are wild no more. But where the sea and land have been left pretty much alone to contend with each other in their inexorable, time-honored ways, the character of the coast is enormously varied. It ranges from placid coves where children hunting for shells in the shallows can dabble safely and the muddy sand is alive with fiddler crabs and other charming creatures to surf-beaten outer beaches where the great untamed ocean rules all things.

The first settlers of the Atlantic seaboard generally avoided beaches and built their villages on some protected harbor or a little way up a river. They did so partly because they feared pirates and other seaborne enemies, but also because they knew that the ocean can be hostile. In my family's house was a box of old land deeds, some of them dating back to colonial times. I remember one of them describing a desirable parcel of land as "standing beyond the reach of the sea." This meant that it was not only well away from the beach but also safe from the far-reaching storm tides that sometimes invade the lowlands behind it. For colonial people the beaches were good for fishing, looking for stranded whales and gathering bits of lumber and other useful flotsam. I am sure some individuals tramped the beaches simply to enjoy their beauty and freedom, but they had too much good sense to build their houses on or near these battlegrounds.

Beaches are no less hazardous now than they ever were (except for the absence of pirates), but modern people feel differently about building on them. Land on an accessible beach not too far from a large city is extremely valuable, and often the beach front is crowded with summer cottages, their eaves almost touching. In parts of New Jersey the cottages sometimes stand in ranks as many as 20 deep. The dunes are leveled; the beach grass is gone. The beach itself, which is no one's responsibility, is littered with beer cans, papers and garbage. No doubt the people who spend vacations there are happy after their fashion, but the cottages do not last long. Sand blows against the windows, grinding them opaque; woodwork weathers quickly and metal fittings are corroded by salt spray. Even a modest gale can do the cottages damage, and a really great storm may wreck them completely. Nearly all beach-bank developments have been damaged badly at least once, some of them several times. I know a New England beach that has been wiped clean—as clean as when the Indians owned it—by two separate hurricanes, but now it is again thick with ramshackle cottages. The plans of the lots are on file, so if the owner of a storm-destroyed cottage gets discouraged, some real-estate man sells his lot to a newcomer who does not know how vulnerable that beach is to hurricanes.

By great good fortune many of the best beaches along the Atlantic seaboard were not easily accessible until recently. Some were on islands, others on peninsulas whose poor roads made them hard to reach from centers of population. They remained undeveloped long enough for some branch of government to step in and keep them from becoming seaside slums. All along the coast (with the longest gaps in New Jersey) are generous public beaches, most of them as clean and beautiful as they were a century ago, and some of them surprisingly wild. Some are owned by towns or cities, others by states. The biggest and most attractive are the national seashores, operated intelligently and devotedly by the National Park Service.

The northernmost of these clear, clean windows on the Atlantic is the Cape Cod National Seashore, which was authorized by act of Congress in 1961. It takes in the great outer beach on the forearm of Cape Cod, which stretches 30 wind-beaten miles from Provincetown to Nauset. No one knows how glorious a beach can be until he has stood on this one during a winter storm or, perhaps more subtly dramatic, when not the faintest breeze is stirring but immense smooth green rollers are coming in from a storm a thousand miles away and sliding toward the shore like sculptures of polished glass.

The next national seashore down the coast is Fire Island, a narrow 32-mile-long barrier island off the south shore of Long Island, only 20 miles from New York's city limits. It was snatched from the jaws of development in 1964. What saved it was its insularity; it was until the early '60s accessible only by boat. Successful delaying tactics by conservation forces kept a highway from being built along it until the national seashore was established. Many parts of this seashore look much as they did when the first white man, perhaps the first Indian, came to Long Island. Between the small settlements, reached only by ferries, are long stretches of real wilderness: seaside forests, dune land, peat bogs, grassy marshes. Wildlife, including deer, is abundant. The wide beach of fine white sand is a delight. Its thin sprinkling at high-water mark of buoyant man-made flotsam is interesting rather than offensive. Having traveled miles from any source it is as clean as the sea. Once, on an unfrequented part of the beach, I found a wave-worn plastic bottle with two pennies and five glass marbles in it. I thought sympathetically about the child who had wept on losing this treasure, and I left it near a settlement so some other child might find it.

New Jersey has no national seashore; all the way from Sandy Hook at the mouth of New York Harbor to Cape May on Delaware Bay there are just two small state parks. There is, as well, a splendid 19,500-acre national wildlife refuge, but almost all the rest of the state's 127-mile shore front, which is lined with barrier islands, has been uglified by the most reckless kind of real-estate development. In some places crude tarpaper shacks perch on rotting piles in the middle of salt marshes. These were probably built by squatters, but many legally sanctioned developments are hardly better. Almost the entire Jersey coast is an eyesore, although its islands and inlets could have made it one of the most beautiful places in the United States.

Below Cape May begins the Delmarva (Delaware-Maryland-Virginia) peninsula. On its ocean side is Delaware Bay; on the mainland side is Chesapeake Bay. Until 1964, when the Norfolk to Cape Charles bridge-tunnel was built across Chesapeake Bay, the southern end of the peninsula was hard to reach from large cities. Since many of the barrier islands off its coast, with their superb beaches, remained almost uninhabited, acquisition by the government was not complicated. The biggest island, Assateague, whose beach is 37 miles long, has become Assateague National Seashore, which has everything a seaside wilderness should have: salt marshes full of waterfowl; mud flats and shallow bottoms full of shellfish; forests, meadows, dune country. It even has a herd of wild ponies—descendants, some people believe, of a few that escaped from a wrecked 16th Century Spanish ship. The Park Service plans to keep the northern end of the island in its natural wild state, to be reached only on foot or by boat. Most of the southern end is given over to the Chincoteague National Wildlife Refuge, one of the principal stopping places for migratory birds using the Atlantic flyway.

South of Assateague is a whole fleet of islands, the outer ones fringed with delightful beaches. So far they have been little developed. Some are still in private hands, and others have been bought by conservation-minded groups or individuals who intend to protect them from the bulldozers. Two thirds of Hog Island, one of the most attractive islands, has been bought by the Nature Conservancy, whose policy is to

Sea gulls scavenge at the water's edge along a flat New England beach for particles of food left stranded by an ebbing late-afternoon tide.

purchase desirable wild areas when opportunity offers and either hold them or manage them until the federal government or a local government or conservation agency can find funds to take them over.

Perhaps the most extraordinary of the seaside parks along the Atlantic is the Cape Hatteras National Seashore, which keeps in trust most of North Carolina's remarkable Outer Banks. These long, narrow islands look like typical barrier islands, but they do not lie a short distance offshore as the typical islands do. They arch boldly into the Atlantic far out of sight of land. At one point Hatteras Island is 30 miles from the mainland. Pamlico Sound, between island and mainland, is a good-sized inland sea. Driving along the highway that traverses Hatteras and Ocracoke Islands is like taking an ocean voyage.

The national seashores are the biggest of the Atlantic seaside parks and usually the wildest, but between them are smaller islands and lengths of shore, some of them exquisitely beautiful, that are protected from cluttered destruction by some local public agency. Until a few years ago it was considered a foregone conclusion that most of the beaches, and even some salt marshes remaining in private hands, would go the sad way of the Jersey shore. This has not happened. Increasing public pressure has resulted in stricter zoning laws and antipollution regulations that hamper reckless development. The building of seaside slums continues—but at a slower pace. All along the coast a struggle is in progress to put more shorelands under public control so their wild beauty will be preserved.

Beaches do not "just happen" nor are they permanent. They are temporary boundaries that reflect the shifting balance between the land, the sea and the air. A change in any one of these three elements affects the beaches profoundly. If the land rises, as happens frequently on the geological time scale, the beaches may be lifted and stranded far inland. On the other hand, Georges Bank, a great shoal area about 70 miles east of Cape Cod, is a "sunken Nantucket." When sea level was lower 10,000 years ago, before the glaciers of the last ice age melted and released their water, Georges Bank stood high and dry, covered with forest, roamed by land animals, probably including mammoths, and ringed by beaches that slowly contracted as the sea rose until all the land was gone. Even year by year, sometimes day by day, beaches change, and to watch and understand their lively behavior makes them even more fascinating to visit.

The simplest beach is the kind that forms under a bluff of easily eroded rocky material facing the open ocean. Most of the time the waves do not reach the bluff, but when a strong onshore wind is blowing and the tide is high, a few waves touch it now and then, washing down a little of it. Steep places form, and when these are undermined, small avalanches slide to the beach. During storms erosion is faster; great masses fall. Rain nibbles at the slope of the bluff, feeding its substance in driblets to the hungry sea.

Such beaches are generally narrow and contain whatever material is in the bluff—at least for a while. But soon after the stuff falls, the waves start working it over. Fine particles of gravel, clay and silt dislodged by the sea surge stay in suspension long enough to be carried away by currents and eventually deposited in deep, still water. This is why the ocean bottom is usually mud, not sand. Small grains of sand settle faster; they tend to accumulate close offshore. Larger grains along with pebbles stay on the beach until they are moved away.

How are they moved? The answer to this question explains how most of the Atlantic beaches got to be where they are.

Stand on a sandy beach when a high sea is running and watch the surf with something more than passive pleasure and wonder. When a wave rears up and breaks on the beach, notice that its shiny concave face is not clear sea water. It is charged with sand—sometimes enough to make it look brown—that has been loosened by turbulence. When the crest topples forward, crashes in a smother of foam and rushes up the beach, it carries a good part of this sand with it and stirs up other sand. If the waves are parallel to the beach and break on it squarely, most of the suspended sand is washed back by the returning water and deposited near where it came from.

Much more often, however, the waves hit the beach at an angle, and their swash (as their sweep up the beach is called) carries sand up the beach at an angle too. Some of the water sinks into the beach; the rest spreads along it on a short curving course, dragging sand with it as it drains back into the sea. The net result is transport of sand in the general direction that the waves are moving. You can see this happening if you watch closely, and you can measure it after a fashion. Place a small, easily recognized object such as a white pebble on the sand a few feet below the highest level that the waves are reaching and mark its position on the sand higher up. When a wave breaks at an angle, its swash will carry your pebble a little way along the beach (you may lose it, of course), and each successive swash will carry it farther.

Less easy to observe than the sand-carrying swash is the narrow current set up close to shore by waves breaking at an angle. It is strongest in the area of greatest turbulence where the water is thick with stirred-up sand, and it moves that sand along the shore in generous amounts. Abetted by the diagonal swash, this mighty beach builder is called the longshore current.

Whenever waves are hitting a beach diagonally, the longshore current acts like a conveyor belt carrying enormous quantities of sand away from its original source—perhaps the foot of a bluff or a river bringing sand down from eroding uplands. As long as the beach is reasonably straight or curves gently seaward, the sand continues to flow along it, but when the shore curves away from the sea, as at the mouth of an estuary, the sand does not follow the curve but sinks into deep water to form first an underwater sandbar, then a narrow sandspit more or less parallel to the general shoreline. When these conditions prevail long enough, the spit grows into a beach backed up with grass-covered dunes and ultimately into a narrow, forested peninsula extending along the coast. Most of the beautiful broad beaches strung along the Atlantic seaboard grew in this way, starting as slender sandspits deposited by wave-driven longshore currents.

But water currents alone cannot form a beach, part of which stands higher than sea water ever reaches. Once the currents have laid the foundation, the wind takes charge. On sunny, windy days you can see it in action. Stand on the beach when the tide has begun to rise and the part of the beach below high-water mark has had nearly six hours to dry out. Watch the surface of the sand carefully. Especially during gusts you will see a thin film of sand moving with the wind. The individual grains do not rise high; they jump and bounce along, but nevertheless they move, and if the wind is onshore, they soon arrive at a place beyond the reach of the waves even at high tide. Since onshore winds, being unobstructed, are generally stronger than offshore ones, sand tends to accumulate above the high-water mark. Sometimes it forms into dunes that march inland, widening and raising the sandspit until it grows into a peninsula of permanently dry land.

The hero of the next stage is beach grass. The most graceful variety on northern beaches is *Ammophila breviligulata,* a lovely plant with long, narrow fibrous blades that can thrive in pure sand a few feet above high water. As soon as one plant gets rooted, it sends out long, thin stems that run beneath the surface, pushing up tufts of blades every foot or so. Soon the sand is populated with green fountainlike clumps whose drooping blade tips swing in the wind, drawing interlacing circles on the sand. When wind blows into the grass and slows down, much of the sand it is carrying drops to the surface and stays there, accumulating among the clumps of beach grass. This build-up does not bother the grass, which merely grows higher and thicker, developing into a dense mat that catches sand delivered by the wind and builds it into a high bank held together by wiry stems. Often the bank rises 30 feet above high-water mark.

When such a beach bank has been stabilized for a few years, other plants appear among the grass clumps: beach plum, poison ivy, bayberry, beach goldenrod and, finally, oak, pine and other large trees. Often, behind a beach, you will see heavily forested land with steep little hills; these were once moving sand dunes that were stopped in their tracks by beach grass.

When a beach peninsula grows 10 miles long or more, the rising tide takes a considerable time to flow around its tip and fill the bay behind it. Sometimes there may be a difference of several feet between the water level on the seaward beach and that in the bay. During onshore gales when the tide rises unusually high, a great wave may sweep across the peninsula. Finding nothing to oppose it, it runs in a foaming torrent down to the level of the bay, forming a shallow channel. Other waves follow and quickly cut the channel deeper. When it gets deep enough, the ocean races through it like a white-water river. The flow continues until the water in the bay is at the same level as the ocean outside and one end of the peninsula has been cut off to form an island. The many narrow barrier islands that line the Atlantic coast from Long Island southward and are backed by shallow bays, marshes or inland waterways were created in this fashion.

As soon as a new inlet is cut, the longshore current tries to close it with sandspits while tidal currents racing through it try to keep it open. An inlet may close soon after it is formed or it may stay open for centuries. Even when an inlet does not close, its tendency is to move in the prevailing direction of the longshore current. While this sand-carrying current builds up one bank of the inlet, the tide flowing in and out from the sea erodes the opposite bank. Many people who have built houses or wharfs on a channel between two barrier islands have discovered this fact to their sorrow.

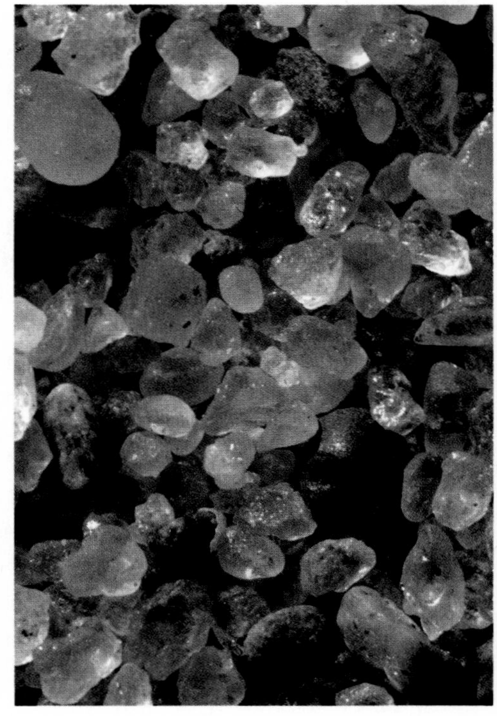

Shown magnified 10 times, granules of sand freshly washed by a retreating tide on Cape Cod reveal a diversity not apparent to the naked eye. The glassy white and yellow grains are composed of quartz; the most common variety of beach sand, they are hard enough when blown about to pit a glass windshield. The rough gray grains are particles of feldspar, and the darkest grains—a brownish red—are garnet.

While a beach peninsula is building higher and extending along the coast, another kind of build-up proceeds in the sheltered bay that it has cut off from the ocean. The tide flows in and out of the bay, and rivers and creeks flow into it from the land. All this water carries suspended material: fine particles of clay and silt, waterlogged vegetation and the shells of tiny marine animals. Much of this settles to the bottom, forming rich mud. Then along the shoreline between high- and low-water marks, a tall salt-resistant grass, *Spartina alterniflora,* begins to grow luxuriantly. Its roots bind the mud together, and with its dead stems ultimately make a mat of fiber that collects silt. Gradually the bottom builds up, and new water-soaked land made of fibrous, springy peat grows out from the shoreline. Other plants find this type of land congenial and their growth raises its level to the high-water mark. This is salt marsh. It is one of the earth's most interesting kinds of terrain, packed with myriad kinds of life. As a sandy peninsula grows across the mouth of an indentation in the coast, a salt marsh usually follows in its shelter, until it often fills the whole bay.

Such is the grand strategy of the growth of beaches. Anyone who walks along the shore can follow it, and a glance at a large-scale map or aerial photograph of the Atlantic coastline shows many results of the process. But beaches also have innumerable small-scale items of interest. The smallest, perhaps, is the sand itself, which varies according to its origin and what has happened to it after it reached the beach.

When loose material falls from an eroding bluff, it generally consists of a gravelly mixture of sand, pebbles and cobbles, as well as some large boulders. The boulders stay where they fall, sometimes forming a point of rocks that reaches out to sea. As the rest of the material moves along the beach on the conveyor belt of the longshore current, it soon leaves behind the cobbles and most of the pebbles, which only violent waves can move very much. Still farther down the beach, the larger sand grains fall out in their turn. At the far end of a long beach the sand is usually fine.

Whether coarse or fine, sand particles are not all alike. When I was a child I used to take some of our Cape Cod sand, which is rather coarse, spread it out on my palm and look for "rubies" in it. Usually I found some: clear red gleaming specks. Sometimes I had a run of luck and collected a lot of them and took them home to admire at my leisure. They were not rubies, of course. They were tiny granules of garnet eroded from crystalline rock and resistant to wear because of their hardness. Recently I looked for them again (with a lens this time because my eyes no longer focus as closely as a child's). They seemed to be scarcer, but I did manage to find a few.

Most of the grains of sand on my home beach are translucent quartz, rather jagged and angular. A few are darker, probably feldspar, which is almost as hard as quartz. The light-colored opaque grains are mostly ground-up shell, which is commoner on beaches farther south where more clams and other shelled creatures are cast ashore. I looked in vain for the black rounded grains that I remember from childhood. I did not really expect to find them; I knew they were made of anthracite coal spilled from a wrecked coal barge. For a while they made interesting streaks of black in the white sand, but they were too soft and light to stay on our beach for long.

Geologists who study sand in a more perceptive way can sometimes trace back the history of individual grains for millions of years. Most grains (not the shelly bits, of course) came originally from once-molten rock that cooled and solidified slowly enough for good-sized grains to exist in it. Granite is a familiar rock of this kind. When it weathers, its angular quartz and feldspar come loose and form angular particles of sand. Feldspar tends to split and chip into fine particles that become components of silt and clay. Quartz is hard and will take a lot of punishment. It is safe to say that most of the quartz grains trodden upon by the dinosaurs 70 million years ago exist somewhere today.

But quartz grains do change, gradually losing their angularity as their sharp corners and edges wear away. A little of this wear happens in rivers that carry fresh grains from eroding mountains down toward the sea; apparently stream-borne grains do not hit together hard enough to erode one another much. Wind-carried grains hit harder, often knocking chips off each other. The dust that results is carried far away by the wind, and the grains are left a little rounder than before.

The jaggedness of most of the sand grains on my Cape Cod beach shows that they are young and have had little rough treatment since they were released from their parent rock. Presumably they weathered out of New England's granite and were transported to Cape Cod by the ice-age glaciers. Quartz grains on beaches farther south are often more rounded and probably much older. They probably left their original rock many millions of years ago and were jostled by wind and water until they came to rest in a sand deposit that got covered by other material and slowly hardened into sandstone. During this time the grains were not destroyed or further altered in shape. When the sandstone was eroded, the grains were released again to be blown by the wind and washed into the sea by water. Grains that have been through several such long, slow cycles are as smoothly rounded as potatoes.

Sand grains have much to do with determining the character of a beach. Where they are coarse, the beach is steep and narrow. As they get finer, the beach becomes wider and flatter. This is because the waves can pick up fine sand more easily, hold it in suspension longer and, as they recede, deposit it farther offshore, building up a wide, gently sloping shelf. Such beaches are generally firm because fine sand sticks together more tightly than coarse sand.

The round of the seasons also influences the character of most beaches, and often alters them considerably. Not all beaches change in the same way, but there is a family resemblance in the seasonal changes that take place on most of the beaches along the Atlantic seaboard. Onshore winds are apt to be stronger in winter than in summer; violent storms are more frequent, and the waves that hit the beaches are higher, steeper and closer together. They deliver more energy and keep the sand stirred up for longer periods. Sometimes they chew at the beach bank, the edge of the dune area behind the beach. More often they do not reach quite so far but carry sand to the foot of the bank and deposit it in a ridge called the winter berm. Much more sand, however, is dragged off the beach by the winter waves, narrowing the beach and building up into rows of sandbars parallel to the coast. When you visit an Atlantic beach in early summer, you will generally find these bars, which appear above water as the tide falls. They are beautifully smooth and many a child loves to play on them, but he should be warned not to linger there too long because the returning tide may leave him marooned on a shrinking island.

In summer the waves are usually gentle. They do not surge as high up the beach and so do not nourish the winter berm, much of which is soon blown away by the wind. They do, however, attack the sandbars, carrying their sand toward shore. Gradually during the summer the sandbars move shoreward, broadening the beach for the storms of the coming winter to tear down again.

Whatever their shape and whatever the season, beaches have fascinating markings on them. The commonest are the waves' swash marks, which are best seen on an ebbing tide early in the morning before human footprints have blurred their outlines. They are long, interlacing curves whose concave sides face toward the sea. The arc of each curve defines the limit reached by an individual wave in its forward surge. Also common are the parallel troughs and ridges called ripple marks. If you find them in dry sand above high-water mark they were made by wind; those lower down were generally made by flowing water. But in both cases these marks were produced in the same way. When water or wind passes over an obstacle, even one as slight as an irregularity in the sand, it turns downward and excavates a trough. The sand thrown up forms a ridge that acts as an obstacle in turn and makes the current excavate another trough beyond it.

Just below high-water mark the sand sometimes shows "pinholes," small holes that look as if they were dug by some small creature. Once I spent some effort trying to find the inmates, but I was wasting my time. Pinholes are caused when the swash of a wave flows in a thin layer over dry sand and the air trapped beneath the sand escapes upward through the weakest places it can find, making the pinholes. But not all the air escapes. When the swash of a second wave flows over the same place, the top inch or so of sand is already saturated and comparatively impervious. When additional air from below tries to escape, it raises the wet sand layer in domes a couple of inches across. They look as if they were made by living creatures, but if you slice them carefully with a knife, you will find they are hollow and uninhabited. There are other beach markings of more obvious origin. These are "rills," which look like miniature branching river systems with their mouths toward the sea. They are formed when water that has saturated the beach at high tide drains out as the tide falls. They branch for exactly the same reason that large rivers do: a tiny channel that happens to be slightly deeper than others near it gets more water and can therefore dig itself deeper still. Then other channels run down into it because it offers the easiest way for their water to get to the sea.

Sometimes a beach has low, curving mounds many feet long and set at regular intervals with their concave sides usually toward the sea. These are called cusps, and they seem to form most frequently when waves have been breaking on the beach at right angles. They are my favorite markings because the experts cannot explain them satisfactorily, and I enjoy this.

A Landscape in Flux

PHOTOGRAPHS BY HARALD SUND

In almost every type of terrain the forces of erosion do their work imperceptibly over tremendous spans of time. But sandy beaches are altered by water and wind at a rate fast enough to be discerned by the human eye. The most pliable and fleeting are the barrier beaches, low-lying strips of sand surrounded or penetrated by the sea. Even the relatively stable beaches of Cape Cod, pictured on the following pages, may change dramatically from one day to the next.

The distinctive character of Cape Cod's beaches was determined by an epochal event that created the Cape itself. As the last ice age waned about 15,000 years ago, immense glaciers, freighted with soil and fragmented rock they had acquired on their advance from the north, melted back, dumping their loads on New England's continental shelf, then a coastal plain.

As the icecaps melted, the water they released slowly raised the level of the sea—perhaps by as much as 300 feet. Then, about 3,500 years ago, Atlantic waves began to chew away at the glacial deposits that formed the original Cape. Since then, the sea has drastically remodeled the Cape, smoothing its ragged coastline by slicing off promontories and filling in bays and inlets with beaches formed of glacial debris.

Three motive forces are involved simultaneously in this continuing process. The backwash of waves sweeps the loose debris from the beach into the surf; coastal currents, acting like a giant conveyor belt, drag the material over the shallow sea bottom along the shore; and from time to time incoming waves hurl debris back up on another beach. In general, large, heavy materials are moved only slowly by powerful waves, while smaller, lighter particles are transported farther and faster. The smallest, lightest grains of sand come briefly to rest near the water's edge, then are washed back into the current or are blown up the beach by the wind to build dunes.

Accumulating like snowdrifts at the back of the beach, dunes can pile up in a succession of windy winters to heights of 50 feet or more; often they are given a semblance of permanence by the beach grass and bushes that take root in them and help to stabilize the shifting sands. Even so, a long line of dunes that has dominated the inland side of a beach for centuries can be leveled —overnight—by a severe storm.

The basic components of a beach—and the primal force that forms it—are combined in this picture. In the remote past each sand grain was, like the pebble, a piece of a larger rock. Worn down by their water-borne travels, the sand grains become so small and light that they may be moved down a coast from beach to beach for centuries with little further reduction in size.

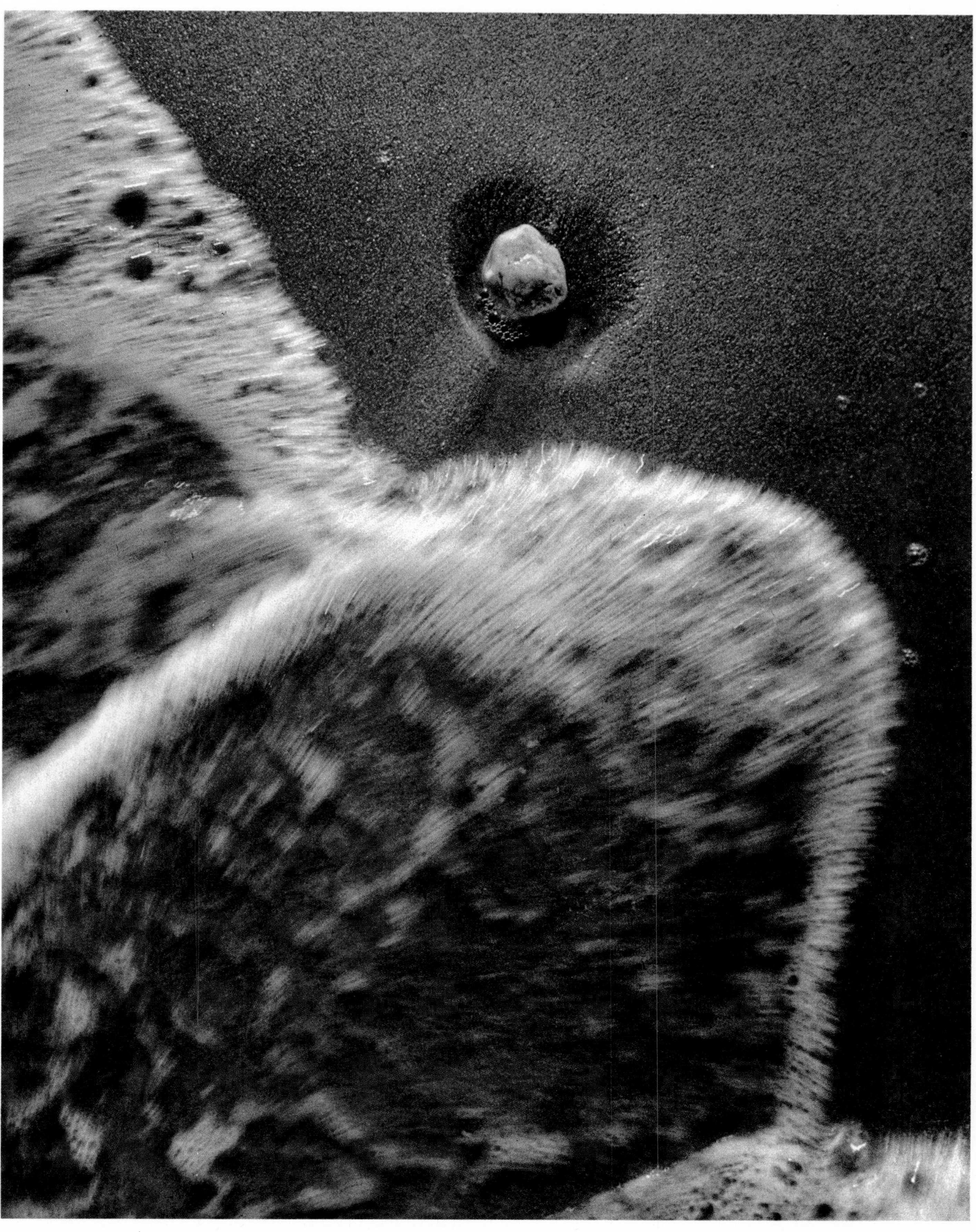

Feeder of Beaches: A Glacial Dump

Cape Cod's coastal moraine—a long, broad ridge of glacial debris—is hundreds of feet thick, and in some sections of the coast it takes the form of long, massive bluffs that rise as much as 180 feet above the beach. But for all their solid, fortresslike look they are highly vulnerable to the pounding of waves whipped up by the region's nor'easters; these fierce storms slam into the New England coast after an unimpeded run of more than 300 miles from their breeding grounds off Nova Scotia. Battered by storm waves that exert as much as 6,000 pounds of pressure per square foot, the many bluffs that stud the Cape Cod shoreline have loosed huge amounts of debris, thus contributing to the process of beach building farther along the coast. In so doing they are contributing to their own doom. Although rates of erosion have varied considerably in the past, some geologists estimate that at the present rate—about three feet of coastline per year—the towering bluffs of Cape Cod's Great Beach are now about halfway to dissolution, and may completely disappear in about 5,000 years.

At the Great Beach near Truro, tons of raw material destined for other Cape Cod beaches repose in a high seaside bluff, its profile kept steep by the action of undermining waves. According to one 19th Century study, a 14-mile stretch of these bluffs yielded about 30 million cubic yards of glacial debris to Cape beaches over a 40-year period.

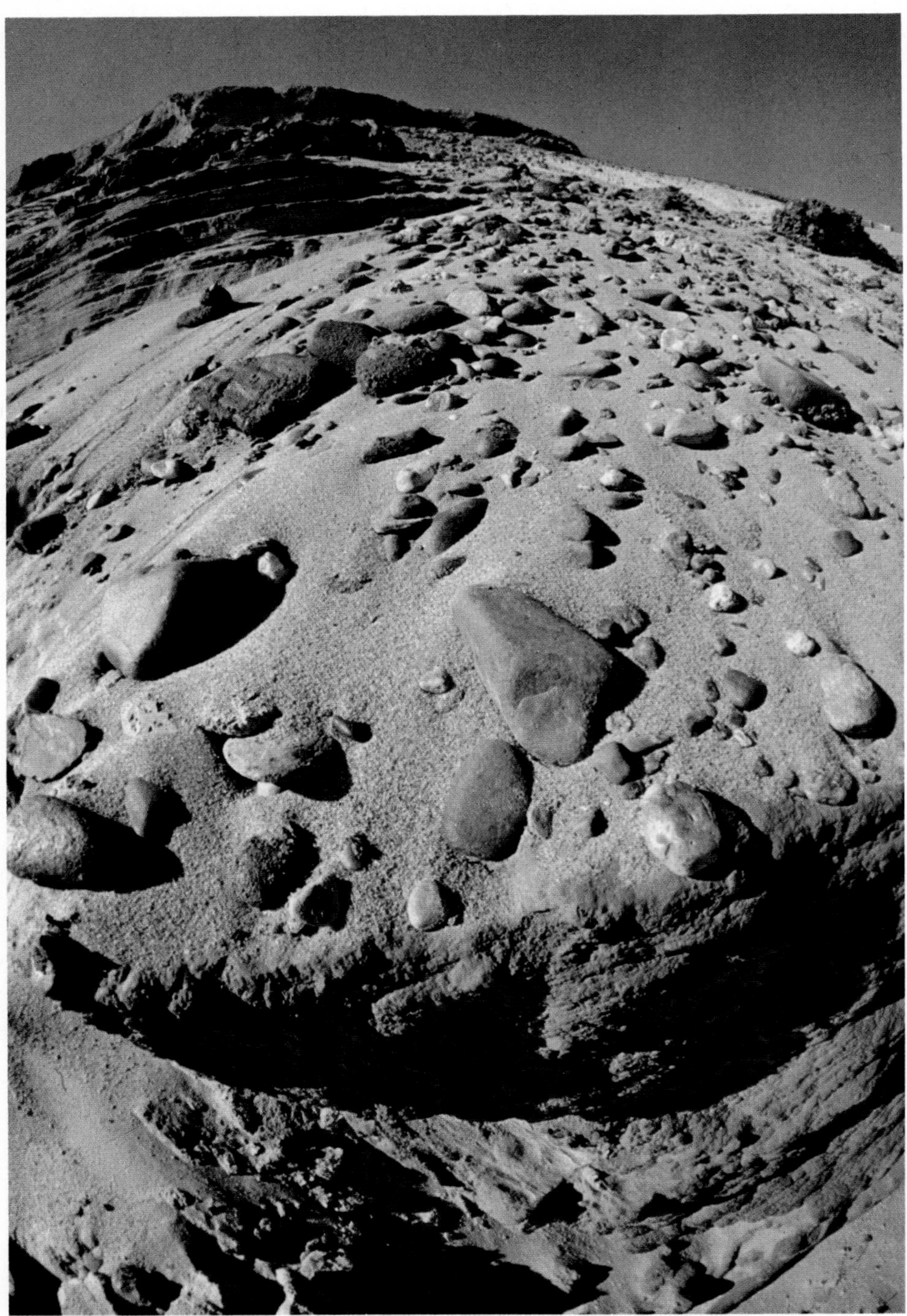

A Loose and Vulnerable Consistency

A moraine deposit is a kind of rocky pudding, a mixture of materials that geologists call glacial till. The chief ingredient of this pudding is sand. A typical grain of sand is a roughly rounded fragment of hard quartz that measures about 1/32 of an inch in diameter. Highly resistant to pressure and weathering, the sand grains—along with clay and silt—lend some cohesion to the mass, yet keep it loose enough to yield readily to the action of waves or wind.

The upper portions of a deposit lie above the level of most waves but are susceptible to the movement of an offshore wind. The smallest, lightest materials—sand grains and silt particles—are first to respond to a breeze. As the sandfall gains momentum, it sweeps pebbles and larger rocks down the slope to the base of the moraine, adding to the quantities of loose debris that will be subject to wave action during high tides or storms. Thus a steady supply of beach-making material always lies within reach of the sea.

A view across the top of a bluff (left) shows the varied size and composition of its parts. These components range from clay and silt particles less than 1/500 of an inch in diameter to granite boulders the size of a small house.

Launched by a gentle breeze blowing from the land side of a Cape Cod glacial deposit, sand cascades down the moraine's terraced face. The graceful streams of sand are flecked with glistening particles of mica.

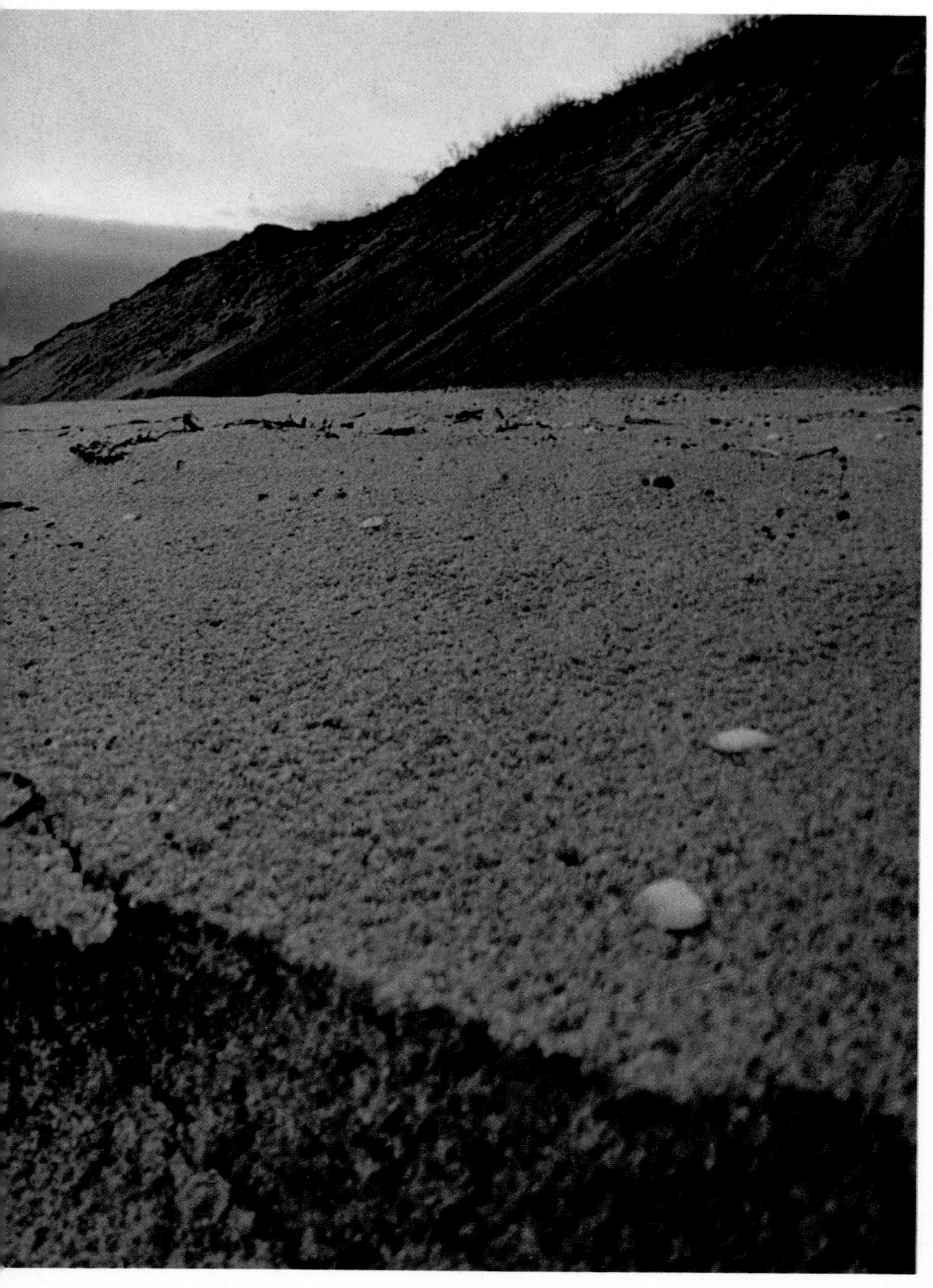

Separating the Sand from the Rocks

The miscellaneous materials pried loose by wind and wave are subject to a continuous sorting process. The backwash of the waves starts things off—separating the lighter from the heavier materials as it drags the debris into the surf. Here coastal currents take over, sending sand farthest and fastest along the shore and pebbles not quite so far. Under storm conditions the currents also move cobbles a considerable distance, although not so far as the pebbles.

The surf on a particular beach carries the sorting process further, selectively hurling the transported materials up on the beach roughly according to size and weight. The finest grains of sand, so light that wave action washes them easily up and down the beach, are concentrated on the foreshore near the water's edge. More powerful waves with a longer reach distribute larger, heavier materials behind the foreshore in a terracelike ledge called a berm. Some broad, well-developed beaches have several berms that range inland in a series of ascending steps. The berm farthest from the sea is always created by the most powerful of the winter storm waves.

A stretch of beach near Highland Light reveals a steep, ledgelike berm, piled up by the action of powerful winter waves that dump their debris well beyond the level reached by normal tides. The foreshore at left below the berm has a lower slope built of materials deposited by gentler waves.

The Power of Moving Sand

Given a good onshore wind and a quick drying at ebb tide, the fine sand ordinarily left on the foreshore by wave action may not stay there long; it is likely to be blown farther up the beach. Once airborne, sand grains go bouncing inland like tiny billiard balls, knocking other grains into the path of the wind. Gathering in clumps of grass germinated from wind-blown seeds, the grains accumulate on flat open stretches; over a period of several seasons they may build dunes that on Cape Cod have reached as high as 150 feet.

Under the impetus of the prevailing wind, the sand dunes at the tip of the Cape move cross-country in a southeasterly direction. Periodically, their progress is arrested, especially in spring and summer when the wind abates; if a dune remains motionless long enough, it may be overgrown and held in place by patches of fast-spreading vegetation *(overleaf)*. But when dunes are on the march, they overpower everything that lies in their path. Slowly but relentlessly they smother salt marshes, devour forests and turn miles of inland terrain into a sea of flowing sand.

Overwhelmed by sand skeletonized pitch pines attest to the might of a moving dune. Although some of the sand has since blown away to reveal the desiccated crowns of the trees, they died soon after the sand completely covered them. Dune-invaded pines can survive only if their tops remain above sand until the dunes move on.

Once restless travelers, sand dunes near Provincetown now are held down by beach grass and such bushes as bayberry and beach plum.

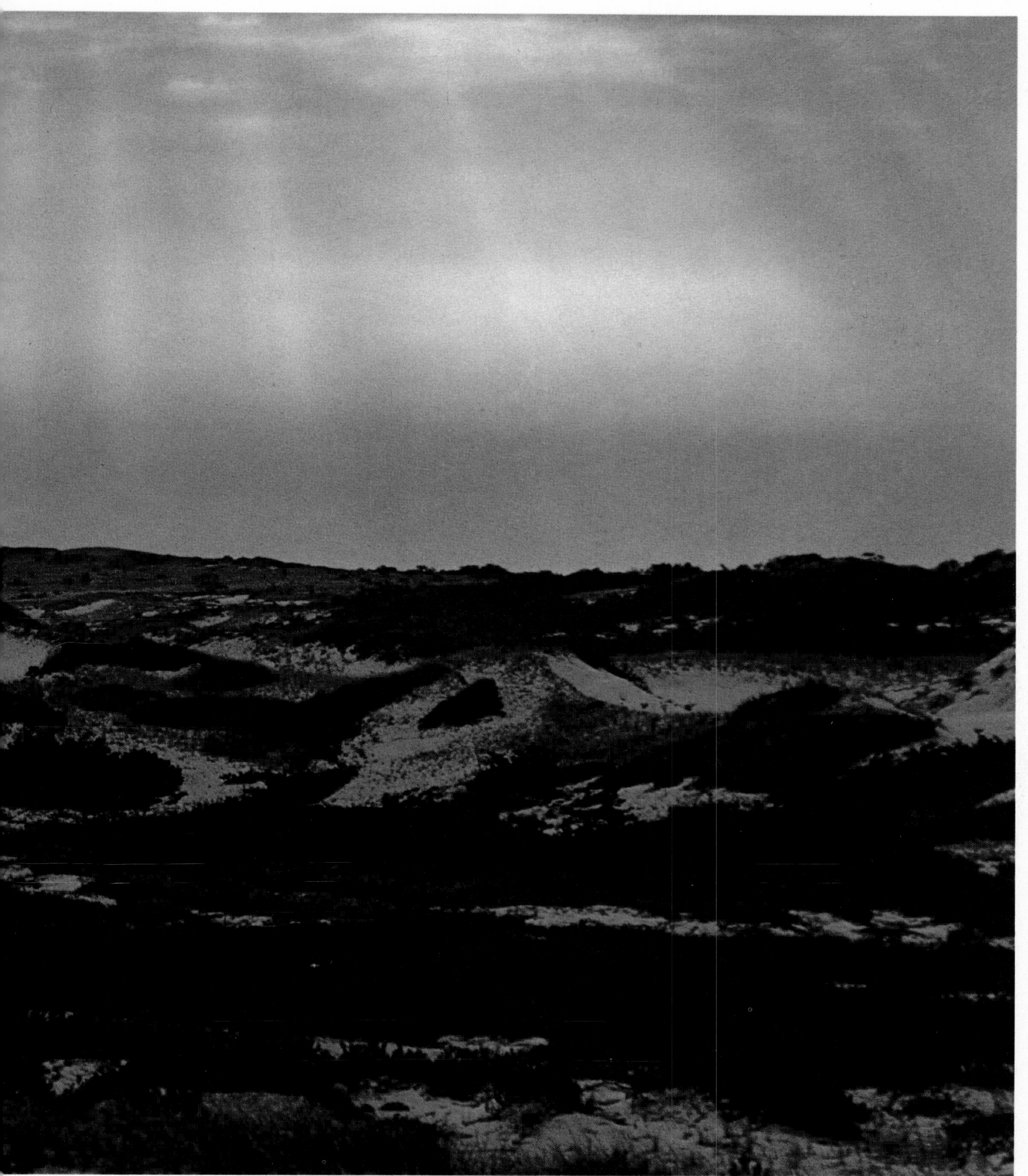

But their stability is tenuous. With any serious break in the fragile net of vegetation, the dunes can resume their cross-country march.

2/ Gifts of the Glacier

Sand is a substance that is beautiful, mysterious, and infinitely variable; each grain on a beach is the result of processes that go back into the shadowy beginnings of life, or of the earth itself. RACHEL CARSON/ *THE EDGE OF THE SEA*

Officially they call it Cape Cod Light, but to most Cape Codders it is still Highland (pronounced *high land*) Light. Its white tower, seven miles southeast of Provincetown and the tip of the Cape, stands on an almost vertical bluff 187 feet above the Atlantic with stark moorlands around it, and since 1796 its steady beam has warned of the terrible beach that growls at the foot of the bluff. When naturalist-writer Henry David Thoreau walked there in the mid-19th Century he shuddered at what he saw. The beach was strewed with the wreckage of ships, surf-chewed bits of their cargoes, pathetic shreds of dead men's clothing. In his book *Cape Cod* Thoreau wrote: "The annals of this voracious beach! Who could write them, unless it were a shipwrecked sailor? How many who have seen it have seen it only in the midst of danger and distress, the last strip of earth that their mortal eyes beheld? Think of the amount of suffering which a single strand has witnessed. The ancients would have represented it as a sea monster with open jaws, more terrible than Scylla and Charybdis."

In Thoreau's day the Great Beach of Cape Cod, which runs an unbroken 30 miles from Provincetown south to Nauset, was a horror that haunted seamen's dreams. The sailing ships that carried New England's exports were forced to round the Cape to reach New York, the Southern states and the West Indies, but they dared not swing far out to sea for fear of the hidden, constantly shifting shoals that lie off that stretch of coast. In foul weather, with a strong onshore wind, giant waves foamed over the shoals with killing force and, abetted by the wind, drove a vessel shoreward. So the ships would wait in Boston or Provincetown Harbor for a favorable wind, then scurry southward along the dreaded beach, their crews praying the weather would hold. Usually it did, or seafaring New England would have been depopulated. But all too often the sky turned dark, and a howling nor'easter stirred the sea into hissing whitecaps. In the gale a little white-winged ship was almost helpless. Desperately it would try to claw away from the beach, but could not gain against the wind. Its rigging would part, its sails carry away. Walls of green water would surge over the sides, washing men from their stations. The ship would come closer and closer to the breakers on the beach. At nightfall the spark of Highland Light would shine like a single star above the roaring blackness. If it stood high, the seamen would curse it, for it showed how near they had drifted to shore.

At last the awful moment would come when the keel struck hard on a sandbar. The vessel would swing into the trough of the sea and strike again and again. The deckhouse would go overboard and some of the sailors with it. The heavy timbers of the hull would snap like twigs. The masts would fall. The cargo would spill out: bolts of cloth, boxes of codfish, barrels of Medford rum. A few of the men might reach the beach alive, but death often awaited them there: the surf raged against the bluff, permitting no man to climb it.

Such was the Great Beach of Cape Cod in the years of sail. It claims few victims now. Small and middle-sized craft avoid it entirely by using the Cape Cod Canal. Freighters and tankers too large to get through the canal have ample power to keep their distance from the beach in the dirtiest weather. Today the white contrails of jet liners headed for Europe are a commoner sight than sails.

But the beach is just as dramatic as in Thoreau's time. The sea still beats relentlessly, sometimes with short, steep breakers, sometimes with long, widely spaced swells that may have come all the way from Spain. Long stretches are as unfrequented as they were when Thoreau imagined himself "traversing a desert." He wrote: "The solitude was that of the ocean and desert combined. A thousand men could not have seriously interrupted it, but would have been lost in the vastness of the scenery as their footsteps in the sand." A century later no footprints mar that sand; no houses are visible above the bluff. A man who does not mind walking can still be alone with the sand and the sea.

Recently I gave a lift in my car to two engaging girl hikers from Connecticut who said they were looking for a really deserted beach. I was planning a walk northward from Highland Light, so I took them there and showed them how to get down the bluff by way of a precipitous gully. Neither the light nor its surrounding buildings were visible from the beach, and there were no signs of human life. The girls ran to the water's edge to dip their bare feet in the rushing foam. "I can't believe it!" cried one of them, waving her arms at the ocean. "All this, and nothing! Nothing at all but us!"

Dressed for a walk along Cape Cod's Great Beach, Henry David Thoreau, naturalist-philosopher of the mid-19th Century, holds his neatly furled umbrella and serviceable valise in a contemporary sketch—the only full-length drawing of the well-known writer—by his friend Daniel Ricketson.

The Great Beach of Cape Cod and all the lovely shore from Boston to New York City are a departing gift from the great continental glaciers of the Late Pleistocene ice age. Cape Cod itself, as well as Nantucket, Martha's Vineyard and Long Island, did not exist until about 10,000 years ago. At that time the ice sheet finally retreated, leaving behind the moraines—great ridges of clay, sand, stones and boulders it had collected elsewhere—that form the shore's framework.

Two of these major moraines along the Atlantic coast show up strongly on topographical maps. The so-called Ronkonkoma Moraine, marking the farthest visible southerly advance of the ice, runs from west to east along the center of Long Island to its eastern tip at Montauk Point, from which it provides the material that forms the 32-mile-long stretch of Fire Island off the south shore. At Montauk Point the moraine dives under the ocean, reappears briefly as Block Island and again as Martha's Vineyard and Nantucket. A second moraine, built by a later glacial advance that did not reach quite as far south, follows the north shore of Long Island and enters the sea at the northern branch of the island's "fishtail." It forms a chain of islands that nearly closes Long Island Sound at its eastern end, touches Rhode Island briefly, then submerges again to reappear as the Elizabeth Islands southwest of Cape Cod. This moraine also forms the east-west part of Cape Cod's "arm."

The Lower Cape, the north-south "forearm" that is edged in part by the Great Beach, had a somewhat different origin. To the east of the present coast was another glacial arm that geologists call the South Channel Lobe. This was paralleled on the west by a lobe that had flowed into Massachusetts Bay. These lobes transported debris that filled the narrow trough between them with an "interlobate moraine," a ridge that now stands above the sea as the outermost part of Cape Cod.

The material in these moraines ranges in size from microscopic particles of clay to boulders as big as cottages; it is loosely packed, for it has not had time since the ice retreated to be consolidated into stone. When such a moraine is exposed to the full brunt of ocean waves, it erodes quickly and supplies great quantities of sand to form beaches. Most of Cape Cod's finest beaches trace their origin to the interlobate moraine of the Lower Cape. The sand of the splendid island and peninsula beaches that extend for miles along the south shore of Long Island came from the eroding bluffs where the Ronkonkoma Moraine pokes into the ocean at Montauk Point.

Innumerable books have been written about Cape Cod, ranging from weighty works on glaciology to twittering effusions by connoisseurs of quaintness. My own favorite is Thoreau's book. It first appeared in 1864, and as a practical guide it needs a good deal of updating. But for vivid language and keen observation it has never been equaled.

When Thoreau tramped the Lower Cape, it was a wild, forbidding land, in places an almost lifeless desert. The Pilgrim Fathers, who had sheltered in what is now Provincetown Harbor in 1620 and briefly explored the inner shore of the Lower Cape, had written of flourishing forests there, but these did not last long. Early Cape settlers felled the larger trees for timber or fuel and started fires that burned the ground bare. They plowed the thin, sandy soil to plant crops that were good at first, then worse and worse as the soil gave out. Next the settlers raised cattle and sheep, which ate every sprig of vegetation they could get their teeth into. Loose sand appeared on the surface of the ground; it moved with the wind, formed into steep-fronted dunes (as it still does near Provincetown) and marched cross-country, destroying everything it encountered. The wind swept so fiercely across the unobstructed ground that apple trees 20 years old grew only five feet tall though their branches might spread 18 feet horizontally. For generations miles of the Lower Cape lay abandoned. Most of the few remaining inhabitants were fishermen who huddled around small harbors.

Thoreau has much to say about this man-made desert, but his chief interest was the Great Beach, which he in fact named, and along which he plodded in all kinds of weather. Occasionally he seems to have encountered more people than can be met today on the less accessible stretches. Most of them were wreckers who patrolled the water's edge pulling planks from the surf, extracting iron fastenings from fragments of broken ships, looking for anything that could be used or sold. When ships broke up on the bars, as happened frequently, the local people did all they could, which was usually little, to save the crews; but if there were no survivors they made off with anything that came ashore.

Even the boards carrying the ships' names, which had no commercial or practical value, were salvaged and held in gruesome esteem. Some Cape Cod houses had several of these often intricately carved relics of disaster nailed to their shingled sides.

Books about old-time Cape Cod often refer to "moon cussing." This picturesque term, which I suspect is of "off-Cape" origin, means luring ships ashore on dark, moonless nights by setting up false lights. I doubt that this ever happened. The seamen could easily distinguish such flickering lights from those of the lighthouses, which shone strongly and steadily, and they knew only too well that no harbor existed into which they might be tempted to run for shelter. More likely the worst the Cape Codders did was to appropriate valuable cargo that still legally belonged to a ship or its underwriters.

Wrecking, of course, can be a wildly exciting experience, as I know personally. Years ago, when I lived at Sandwich near the northern end of the Cape Cod Canal, word spread through town early one morning that off the canal's mouth a Canadian boat carrying paper pulp had rammed a British freighter from India. Along with a lot of other people I hurried down to the beach. The rammed ship was not sinking or drifting ashore, but she had a great hole in her hull. Cargo and fuel oil were spilling out and moving into the surf on a stiff onshore wind. First to reach the breakers were large cases of badminton rackets made in India. Eager hands were waiting for them though the rackets were badly damaged by sea water. Then came dozens of large Oriental rugs that flopped sluggishly in the oily surf like weary sea monsters. They were saturated with thick black fuel oil in which sand was embedded, and they were much too heavy to be got ashore by hand. Presently a couple of tractors arrived and dragged a lot of them into the dunes behind the beach. Some of the rugs were claimed by representatives of the underwriters, but others were said to have reached concealment in abandoned chicken houses or under barn floors. I have heard that later they were washed in barrels of kerosene and made as good as new.

Also among the flotsam were some good-sized boxes of blanched almonds; they were badly soaked but their packing had resisted fuel oil. Since no one seemed interested in claiming them, I lugged about 300 pounds of them back to my car. That noontime I spread them out in the sun to dry, and my wife canned a lot of them in glass jars. They kept beautifully. For years our household had almonds in every form, from plain or toasted to macaroons and marzipan.

No lives were lost in that wreck, but in Thoreau's time it was not uncommon to find a corpse tossing in the surf many miles from the scene of a disaster. Thoreau inspected some of these sea-battered remains on the Great Beach. "Close at hand," he wrote, "they were simply some bones with a little flesh adhering to them . . . but as I stood there they grew more and more imposing. They were alone with the beach and the sea, whose hollow roar seemed to be addressed to them, and I was impressed as if there was an understanding between them and the ocean. That dead body had taken possession of the shore and reigned over it as no living one could."

There are no such sad sights along the Great Beach now, and to walk on it is not grisly but exhilarating—an encounter with seaside wilderness at its best. The first time I walked the beach at length was some years ago, during a balmy week in late May. I equipped myself with food in a haversack and two quarts of water in a canteen that an ancestor had carried in the Civil War, and started my walk at the southern end of the beach, near Eastham. It was just as Thoreau had described it, an enormous extent of sand and surf backed by dunes and beach grass and reaching as far as the eye could see. The waves were a rhythmic roar at my right. Little sandpipers ran ahead of me on matchstick legs. These alert brownish-gray birds—named for the piping notes they utter—are seasonal visitors to the Cape, sojourning there from early spring until June on their way north from South America to subarctic breeding grounds. As I watched them darting after a retreating wave to snatch a tiny crab or some other delicacy from the wet sand before the next wave broke, I remembered having heard that if a man could move his legs as fast as a sandpiper, he would be able to cover 100 yards in five seconds. Over my head wheeled graceful herring gulls and their relatives, the terns. I rejoiced in their cries, so much wilder than the songs of birds that nest inland. Many of the gulls were probably year-round residents of Cape Cod, but the terns, distinguished by their sharp, pointed bills and forked tails, may have migrated thousands of miles, from as far south as Brazil.

Although I met no people at all on the beach, for a while three porpoises followed me just beyond the surf, matching their pace to my slow tramping and occasionally standing high out of the water to look me over. After a time they decided I was not worth further attention and took off at cruiser speed.

A little farther on I came upon a large dead shark, partly buried in the sand. It must have been about eight feet long. Its leathery skin was torn in several places, probably by a raccoon or a dog since it was too tough for gulls to have ripped. Finding a shark on a beach is not uncommon; many are caught in the nets of commercial fishermen, and before their thrashing and slashing can damage the nets and let other fish escape they are killed with guns carried for that purpose. Then, having no market value, they are allowed to drift ashore.

Elsewhere in the sand I found half a dozen angler fish, probably also caught in nets and rejected as worthless. Some people call them fishing frogs, but on Cape Cod they are known as monkey fish. They are a mottled brown, about two feet long, flattish and broad at the front end. Their enormous mouths occupy almost the full width of their faces and are filled with sharp, backward-pointing teeth. From above the mouth sprouts a thin rod a few inches long with a small, leaflike tip that the fish waves to lure its prey.

Monkey fish make their living by snuggling down in the sand or mud of the sea bottom until they are almost covered, then wiggling the "bait" at the end of their "fishing rods." When a small fish investigates the bait, the voracious monkey fish bursts out of hiding and sucks the prey into its toothy jaws.

As I walked I noticed, as Thoreau had, that objects far ahead on the beach seemed large until I approached them; then they diminished to tangles of seaweed or chunks of driftwood. The driftwood, in particular, was a delight to contemplate up close—remnants of planks and timbers and piling, stubs of roots and branches of trees, presumably washed down distant rivers into the ocean and now redeposited on this shore. Much of the wood had been bleached gray by the sea and buffed to a satiny finish by the sand, and some roots and branches were contorted into fantastic or decorative shapes that a collector would prize. I especially remember one fairly large root that from a short distance bore a startling resemblance to a man reclining on the sand, his head raised as though watching something at sea and one motionless, many-fingered arm pointing dramatically at the empty ocean. No longer widely used by Cape Codders to warm their houses, the driftwood had had time to accumulate.

Recently I retraced a good part of that walk of years ago, with a purpose in mind: to get a precise demonstration of how beaches are formed. The part of the Great Beach from which I set out—the southern end, near Eastham—is a sandy peninsula that parallels the shore. It is backed by low dunes that the sea had broken through during storms of the pre-

Cap Cook Cast a Way on Cape Cod 1802

An early 19th Century painting shows storm surf rolling the dismasted East Indiaman Ulysses to its doom on Cape Cod's Great Beach.

ceding winter, and behind the dunes is an expanse of salt marsh that has grown in their shelter. On the beach itself the sand was almost entirely free of pebbles—evidence that it had been carried a considerable distance from where it had eroded from the interlobate moraine that forms the Cape's outer shore.

Northward along the Great Beach the pebbles became more numerous and still farther north they were joined by fist-sized stones. This mixed material meant that I was coming closer to the eroding moraine. Then the moraine itself appeared; instead of dunes behind the beach, there was a low but steep bluff of brownish earth with pebbles and stones embedded in it. The sand near the bank was yellowish gray and mixed with clay; the surf had not yet had time to sort its particles according to weight and size and toss them clean. Awash in the surf was a dark boulder, the only boulder in sight. It must have been very hard stone; it had traveled perhaps from as far as Maine, and had resisted the grinding that had destroyed other boulders that had started the journey with it. Now it was standing up to the surf and apparently surviving. I saluted it and wished it well. If it can last a few more decades, the beach will erode westward and leave it peacefully on the sea bottom, below the worst of the wave action.

Thoreau noted that everything the surf gets in its grasp becomes rounded like the stones and pebbles on the beach. He mentioned seeing rounded chunks of peat, rounded fragments of glass, even a rounded cake of castile soap, no doubt from a wrecked ship. I added to his list: a rounded concrete block and a large rounded piece of dark gritty material like blacktop paving. Not far from Nauset Light near where my walk began I had found a bright-red rounded brick. I figured it had been the ballast of a lost lobster pot, but a little farther on I found a similar brick. For miles along the shore the bricks appeared, becoming less rounded. Coming at last to the moraine, I saw on the face of the bluff a section of brick house foundation 10 feet across: a smaller section lay halfway across the beach. Some ill-advised person must have built a house on the edge of the bluff, unaware that it erodes at the rate of about three feet per year. A good many years before, the front part of the foundation had been undermined and started sliding down the beach; the longshore current had carried its bricks, rounding them as they traveled, all the way to Nauset Light.

The farther north I walked, the higher the bluff became, and the steeper and narrower the beach. At last I reached Highland Light, where the bluff is at its highest and is nearly perpendicular, and where the waves at high tide foam against its foot even on calm days. This point marks a sort of divide. Beyond it the sand and other material washed out of the Cape's interlobate moraine tend to move northward, carried by a longshore current propelled by occasional southeast winds. Past the light the bluff stops abruptly, but the beach continues. The "fist" of the Cape that curls into Massachusetts Bay near Provincetown is a giant sandspit still actively building.

The Lower Cape is no longer the bleak, forbidding place it was in Thoreau's time. In many places the forest that the Pilgrims saw is coming back. More than a century ago native pitch pines were planted systematically among the moving dunes, sometimes by sowing the seeds like corn in plowed furrows. For years they grew only a few feet tall but produced seeds that were carried by the wind to sprout in bare places. Slowly humus accumulated among them; other plants took root in their shelter. Oaks reappeared, some of which have reached respectable size. Now most of the Lower Cape is green again, a happy example of how a pleasant land that was wrecked by man's mistreatment can heal itself if given a chance.

It is likely that the Lower Cape will stay green and its beaches will remain beautiful. The reason is the creation of the Cape Cod National Seashore, established by Congress in a fit of farsightedness in 1961—just in the nick of time. Cape Cod had been prized as a summer resort for a century, but the first people who came were rich and therefore few. Their numbers were nothing like the human flood that descended on the Cape after fast roads were built and nearly every American family had acquired a car. Many beaches disappeared beneath close-set cottages. Marshes were dredged and filled; bridges were built to islands and peninsulas that were formerly hard to reach. Pleasant country lanes turned into clogged shopping streets lined with hamburger stands, miniature golf courses and loud discotheques, many of them run by "snow birds," people who take their businesses with them to Florida in winter. But within the boundaries of the seashore, which is under the jurisdiction of the National Park Service and runs from Provincetown to Chatham—and thus includes all of the Great Beach—there has been no development for 10 years.

Even outside the boundaries of the seashore, Cape Cod has many other superb beaches, and most of those that are still unspoiled belong to Cape towns, which operate them as parks. Perhaps because of the example set by the seashore, the towns are devoting considerable effort to keeping their beaches as natural as possible. So in spite of ever-increasing population pressure, Cape Cod's beaches seem to be in no immediate danger. Even Thoreau would enjoy walking on them.

The sandy beaches on the south shore of Long Island boast length and straightness that rank them among the world's best. They have a family resemblance to those of Cape Cod: their sand comes from an eroding moraine and is carried to them by a longshore current. But there are differences. In contrast to the uniform whiteness of the sand on Cape Cod's beaches, the sand on Long Island's beaches is occasionally varicolored because it has been ground out of different kinds of rock. The beaches are longer and straighter than Cape Cod's because the current has an almost straight run of more than 100 miles along the shore. More important than the geological differences are the sociological ones. Long Island is near the world's largest center of population: Metropolitan New York. Nowhere else on earth do so many people live who own automobiles and are therefore able to reach and destroy by their sheer numbers any tract of natural environment that is not well protected. Many once-beautiful Long Island beaches have already been turned into deserts of blacktop and litter. Others are more subtly threatened: they are rapidly washing away because of the adverse effects of ill-considered engineering works.

Relatively remote from the city's grasp, at the eastern tip of Long Island, is Montauk Point. It is here that the Ronkonkoma Moraine, chief source of sand for the island's south shore, enters the ocean. Montauk's slowly eroding bluffs are not as high as those at Cape Cod's Highland Light, but they have their own special element of drama: to reach them, the waves that foam against their base must first cross veritable fields of seaweed-covered boulders. On the easternmost point of land is Montauk Light, the site of whose original tower was selected by President George Washington in 1796. The Father of His Country was something of an engineer, and he must have been aware of the batterings Montauk Point had to endure, for he prudently ordered the lighthouse set some 300 feet back from the encroaching sea. Though erosion has narrowed the safety margin and the present tower stands closer to the tip of the point, it may not have to be moved before the 200th birthday of Montauk Light.

When the last glacier melted and the sea rose to its present level, the hilly region around Montauk Point was an island separate from the rest of Long Island and considerably bigger than it is now. The waves went to work on it promptly, washing its mixture of boulders, stones, pebbles, and sand and clay particles into the surf and sorting them by size and weight. The boulders stayed pretty much where they fell to form a "lag" deposit, part of which is still visible. Smaller chunks of stone moved slowly westward, shifted only by violent storms and becoming strikingly rounded and still smaller. Pebbles moved faster and farther, and the sand started its long ride on the wind-driven current that would carry some of it 130 miles to New York Harbor.

All sorts of interesting things came out of the moraine at Montauk. The glacier that formed it had, in crossing what is now Connecticut, picked up rocks full of magnetite and garnet as well as the usual quartz. Magnetite, an iron compound—a variety of it is the black lodestone once used to magnetize compass needles—can be picked up with a magnet, which is fun to do with a sample of darkish Long Island sand. Garnet is translucent and usually reddish. Large pieces are valued as semiprecious gems, but most garnet granules are no larger than specks of sand. Professor C. L. McCormick of Southampton College, who was my guide to the Montauk region, showed me a dark red boulder whose surface literally glittered with little close-set garnets. The sand in which it was embedded was red and glittering too.

Quartz is lighter than both magnetite and garnet, so when waves carry their grains to a beach, the heavier minerals tend to settle out while the lighter quartz is carried away. Many Long Island beaches and dunes reveal the presence of magnetite and garnet in streaks of pink, red, gray or black sand. I suppose if I had been brought up a Long Islander instead of a Cape Codder, I would never have collected the garnet "rubies" I found in the sand of my hometown beach. They would have been too common.

As opposed to the plethora of garnets, I missed on Long Island the "lucky stones" (my father used to call them "Unitarian holy water") that are so common on Cape Cod. These are pebbles that retain some of the quartz that streaked the parent rock; the prettiest are encircled by veins of pure white quartz. I collect them to stow away in places such as my car or typewriter, where their benign influence is desirable, or to give to friends who may be in need of a change of luck. I have also used them to the gratitude of parents marooned on a beach with small, restless children. When told about lucky stones, the kids scurry around looking for them and do not bother the adults all afternoon. The stones are plentiful; the children may collect 50 pounds of them and demand on pain of tears and tantrums that these hoards be carried

Pieces of driftwood, twisted in striking free forms, appear to be growing out of the pebbles on a Cape Cod beach. Cast up on the shore by

powerful waves, these remnants of an uprooted tree have been warped into their present shapes in the course of a seaborne journey.

home. One way to handle this crisis is to tell the children that all the luck in each of their collections can be concentrated in a single stone by choosing the best one and dipping it ceremonially in the sea.

When the sand that eroded from Montauk Point started its journey westward, the first thing it did was to form a sandspit to join "Montauk Island" to the rest of Long Island. This grew into the sandy isthmus that is now traversed by a highway and the Long Island Railroad. Flowing westward in a roughly straight line, the sand closed the mouths of several small bays on the southern coastline of Long Island and created the wide beaches that make Southampton a sumptuous summer resort. The stream of sand continued westward more or less parallel to the shoreline. When the first settlers arrived on Long Island, a low-lying narrow sandy barrier peninsula stretched from Southampton to what is now Jones Beach, not far from the limits of New York City. Between the peninsula and Long Island itself was a series of shallow bays—some more than five miles wide—which were usually brackish because of their distant connection with the ocean. Storm waves sometimes broke through the peninsula and cut inlets, but they quickly closed again and offered little obstruction to the westward flow of sand.

Then, in 1690 a great storm (probably a hurricane) cut an inlet nine miles wide through the peninsula near the western end of what is now Fire Island. The channel, which still separates Fire Island from Jones Beach, has stayed open naturally, though it has narrowed considerably as a result of a sandspit built across it by the flow of sand. The spit, which is still growing westward at the rate of about 200 feet per year, is called Democrat Point—supposedly because of an incident during a cholera scare in the late 19th Century. By then the area was already being used as a summer resort; it had a number of hotels, including one built on the point and called the Surf Hotel. In 1892, responding to news of a cholera epidemic on a transatlantic steamer, New York's Governor Roswell P. Flower ordered passengers headed for New York City to be taken off the ship and quarantined in the Surf Hotel. When the terrified local people tried to block the landing of the potential cholera carriers, the Governor called out the National Guard. He was a Democrat, hence the name of the point. (This is one of those name-origin stories that I only hope is true and not simply a local legend.)

The opening of Fire Island Inlet, as it is now called, cut a swath near the western end of the long sandy barrier peninsula, but at its eastern end the peninsula remained connected to Long Island for almost 250 years more. Then, in 1931 a storm smashed a channel through the peninsula near its eastern end, creating Fire Island. And in 1938 a hurricane opened yet another inlet through the eastern end of the peninsula, into Shinnecock Bay.

Since then these eastern channels have been kept open artificially. Because they proved so convenient for pleasure boats, jetties were built to keep sand from filling them up. The result has been a slowly developing but far-reaching disaster. The new inlets have proved efficient barriers to the westerly flow of sand along the coast. Southampton's beaches have not been affected since they lie east of the new inlets and continue to receive most of their sand from Montauk. If anything, these beaches are wider and better nourished than ever, but it takes only half an eye to see that beaches that lie west of the inlets are undernourished. Their sand is still being carried westward—but it is not being replaced. The shore fronts of Westhampton and Fire Island are washing away at a rate that costs millions of dollars per year in property damage and a great deal more in damage to natural beauty.

A trip along Fire Island graphically reveals this damage. The destruction of the beach is not uniform. In a few places it is still comparatively wide and backed by gently sloping sand dunes with flourishing beach grass on them. This means that at that particular point the beach is at least holding its own. The grass may catch more sand, and the dunes may grow in height. But in all too many places the beach is narrow and the dunes have steep, concave faces with no grass growing on them or in front of them. Deprived of its natural load of sand from the east, the longshore current is taking sand from the beach and driving the shoreline inland. It is by no means inconceivable that this process may eventually reduce the whole of Fire Island and the beaches between it and New York City to mere sand dunes a few feet above the sea. Indeed it may destroy long stretches of beach entirely, exposing the bays and permitting storms to batter their shorelines.

The people who own summer houses in the dozen-odd small communities stretched thinly along the length of Fire Island try everything possible to stop the erosion that is nibbling at their property. Some of the wealthier communities fortify their beach fronts with massive sea walls of stone and concrete or spend hundreds of thousands of dollars dredging sand from the sea to pile in front of their houses. Often the first good storm carries it all back. At Point O'Woods, the richest community, a big old club is making its last stand with the waves breaking close to its rock-piled foundation.

The conventional way to combat beach erosion is to build groins: short jetties of heavy stone at right angles to the shore. Acting like dams, they catch sand and widen the beach for a short distance on the side from which the sand flow comes (and therefore protect property behind it), but the beach on the other side is correspondingly deprived and wastes away all the more rapidly. More and more groins must be built downcurrent, and they catch less and less sand. Even when an entire beach is studded with groins, the effect is only temporary. Eventually the spaces between the groins become empty and the waves begin again to push back the shoreline.

Worse than groins in their long-term effect are the jetties built to preserve such navigable waterways as Shinnecock Inlet. The jetties entirely stop the flowing sand, shunting it into water so deep that even great storm waves cannot pick it up and move it along the coast. A booklet called *Land against the Sea,* issued by the Army Corps of Engineers, tells with admirable clarity how such structures do their damage.

The booklet also describes the remedy, which is usually too expensive for individual owners of beach-front property or for small towns whose beaches, and often the land behind them, are being destroyed because of sand starvation. The only permanent way to save these beaches is to have a dredge suck up sand from the well-nourished beach on one side of an obstruction such as a breakwater and gush it out on the sand-starved side where the longshore current can pick it up. As soon as the flow of sand has been re-established, the narrow beaches grow wider. Beach grass sprouts on their inner edges, and sand collects among its green stems. A line of dunes grows naturally and all is serene again. The main difficulty is to make the builder of the obstruction, which may be the state or federal government, own up to the harm it has done and pay for the dredging.

Though Fire Island is threatened by beach erosion and population pressure from New York's millions, it is not ruined yet, and the fact that it is now a national seashore under the protection of the National Park Service may save it from both dangers. There is no through road that ordinary automobiles can drive on, and the communities are comparatively small and reachable only by boat. Much of the rest of the island is as it was centuries ago, when it was still part of the barrier peninsula. A man who walks a mile along the beach will probably meet no other pedestrian and will see only a truck or two belonging to authorized agencies such as the telephone company. Fire Island is a startling example of what the lack of an automobile road can do to protect bits of true wilderness even when it is near a huge city; without the roar of engines the place has an almost eerie serenity.

Some parts of the island behind the dunes are clothed by odd stands of trees. The largest and best known of these groves is the Sunken Forest, so called because its floor is lower than the dunes between it and the sea. It is now carefully protected as part of the national seashore and is threaded by several paths kept open by the Park Service. No individual treetops can be seen, only what appear to be rounded hills clad with dense vegetation that seems a few inches tall. Actually this solid-looking surface is a forest canopy whose tender growing twigs are continually pruned back by salt spray from the surf and kept trimmed like topiary trees in a formal garden. These are the tops of trees —sassafras, pitch pine, holly and maple—that have trunks up to one and one half feet in diameter and are 35 feet tall. There are also oak trees, which may be a century old.

If one turns away from the beach at any of the long stretches not occupied by a settlement, the wilderness effect is startling. Behind the first line of dunes are other dunes. Signs of human life are almost nonexistent, but the lacy footprints of mice and the even more delicate tracings left by insects wind through the grass and cross the open spaces. Deer live on Fire Island, but are seldom seen in daytime, when they generally hide in thickets. Their characteristic cloven-hoofed prints stand out most clearly in wet places. Rabbits are common, their hopping gait easily identified in their footprints. The tracks of birds are not easy to tell apart, but those of ducks show full webs between the toes while those of gulls are only partially webbed.

Sometimes tracks in the sand tell a tragic story. Once I followed the trail of some small, mousy creature that had gone by not long before. It wavered from grass clump to grass clump, visited small pits in the sand (perhaps dug by the animal itself) and made a tangle of marks among insect remains that may have been leftovers from a hearty meal. Then the tracks led across a stretch of bare sand. Halfway across they ended suddenly in a large, confused blur showing a few big claw marks. A hawk or an owl had accounted for my mouse.

Penetrating the Sunken Forest

PHOTOGRAPHS BY ROBERT WALCH

In colonial times, many of the beaches along the Atlantic seaboard were backed by thick woods. Few are so blessed today, but on Fire Island, only about two hours by car and ferry from New York City, the 75 acres of woodland, bog and salt marsh known as the Sunken Forest have miraculously managed to survive. A dark and brooding domain, this maritime wilderness lies near the island's western end, its southern edge on the Atlantic and its northern edge on Great South Bay, which separates Fire Island from Long Island. Even before this maritime wilderness became a protected part of the Fire Island National Seashore, it had remained pristine partly because no public automobile road ever approached it, partly because the islanders stoutly resisted any attempts to exploit the landscape.

The Sunken Forest is not really sunken, but it seems so because its floor is generally lower than the line of high dunes on its seaward side. It probably got its name from early settlers who glimpsed it first, as most modern visitors do, from the dunes—seeing only the very tops of sizable trees that had been sculptured by salt spray until they were as smoothly rounded as a well-clipped privet hedge. From the dunes, the trees look more like low bushes and give no clue to their actual height, which can be as much as 35 feet.

The approach from the ocean side was the one I, too, chose when I explored the Sunken Forest on a day in early autumn. As I drew near, I could see the salt sea spray coming across the beach. A heavy surf was breaking and tossing droplets of water high in the sun-warmed air. The smallest drops were evaporating before they fell, leaving microscopic crystals of salt that drifted inland as a thin, slightly yellowish haze. This dusting of salt, which kills the tender young growth of most seaside plants, had even cowed some hardy pitch pines behind the first line of dunes; they were creeping along the sand like vines.

Farther inland, in the Sunken Forest itself, the salt spray inhibits the upward growth of the trees; their green tops are therefore more or less even. Standing on the beach and looking across the forest I was reminded of a bunch of broccoli. Many of the rounded crowns were thickly set with salt-bleached dead twigs like porcupine quills. Some trees had entirely lost their battle with the salt; they still stood, but as skeletons

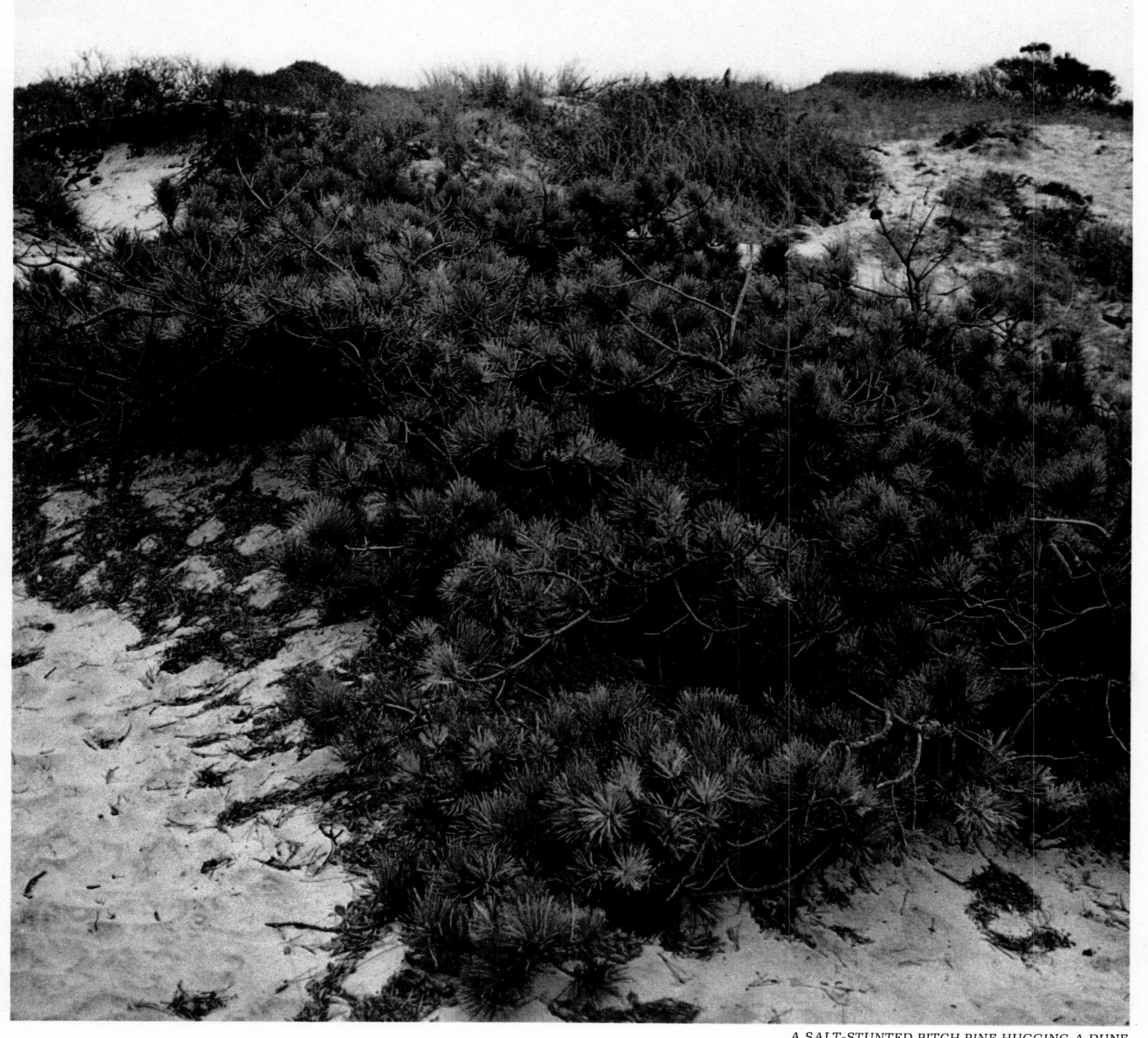

A SALT-STUNTED PITCH PINE HUGGING A DUNE

A MALE MONARCH BUTTERFLY

—dense silvery-gray domes of close-set twiggy thickets supported by twisted limbs.

At the seaward edge of the forest, among clumps of beach grass and the beaten-down pitch pines, I found the pure white sand populated by a few plants tough enough to stand a full dusting of salt. One was bearberry, with its ground-hugging vines that form mats scattered with bright red berries. There, also, were round cushionlike hummocks of beach heather; I regretted having missed their decorative yellow blossoms of spring and early summer. Seaside goldenrod, tolerant of salt, was coaxing magnificent golden plumes from stems rooted in nothing more than plain sand. Circling idly above these hardy plants on the forest's edge was a migrating monarch butterfly, presumably headed south. The bright orange and black of its wings offered lively color competition to beach-plum leaves just beginning to be touched with the russet of fall.

A winding path, which starts at the Park Service ranger station at Sailor's Haven, leads into and out of the forest at its eastern end. Visitors are normally required to stay on the path, to protect both the woods and themselves. I had heard the sad tale of a girl in a sunsuit who strayed from the trail one morning and got lost. When she finally struggled out to the beach, the wilderness had claimed most of her suit and criss-crossed her skin with scratches.

Because I wanted to see and describe the Sunken Forest in more than usual detail, the park rangers permitted me to choose my own route through it, which was more dramatic—and considerably more difficult—than following a path. The first few yards were a tangle of shrubs, a thicket that put up a fight worthy of a barbed-wire entanglement. Some of the dense growth was bayberry with clusters of light gray fruit. Some of it was beach plum, most of whose sweet purplish fruit —each about the size of an olive —had already been eaten by birds.

Under a Green Blanket

Beyond the thicket the interior of the forest was almost dark. Overhead the salt-clipped canopy looked like a green blanket, with sunlight filtering through in occasional thin rays. The tree trunks, from the crooked columns of saplings to the gnarled pillars of mature trees, seldom showed any greenery below their crowns. There were a number of red maples and black gum (also known as pepperidge) trees. But the

THE HEDGELIKE OUTLINE OF THE SUNKEN FOREST

A HOLLY TREE CLIPPED BY SALT SPRAY

two predominant species were holly trees, with smooth trunks up to 15 inches in diameter and crooked branches looking like the upswept arms of candelabra, and sassafras trees, with deeply furrowed bark of a cinnamon brown. The three kinds of sassafras leaves—oval, mitten-shaped with one thumb, and mitten-shaped with two thumbs—were all beginning to show their glorious orange autumn color.

The salt-tolerant sassafras, which is common along most of the Atlantic seaboard, is firmly planted in American history and folklore. The odor of its wood, built into bedsteads, was reputed to ward off bedbugs. The oil of its bark was a basic ingredient of the evil-tasting "spring tonic" administered to children during the 19th Century—but was also used as a perfume in soaps and cosmetics. Sassafras was among the earliest exports of North America. English explorers took back cargoes of its roots, whose aromatic bark was believed to be a cure for almost everything, including what may have been another American export, syphilis. The medicinal reputation of sassafras is now at a low ebb, though the roots are pleasant to chew and

FALLEN SASSAFRAS LEAVES

are still used for making root beer.

Like sassafras, another usually moderate-sized plant—poison ivy—grows tall and rank in the salt air of the Sunken Forest. Along my route a few vines nearly reached the status of trees, measuring more than three inches in diameter. Usually the vines were twined, black and forbidding, up tree trunks, but I noticed some of the largest ones standing alone. Most of their poisonous foliage was visible high in the treetops where the sunlight penetrated.

In the darkest parts of the forest the ground was carpeted with little more than fallen leaves and twigs. But where a tree had blown over or for some other reason the forest canopy was broken to admit sunlight, a hostile undergrowth flourished. Besides poison ivy, it included cat brier, a thorny vine that bears large blue berries and whose leaves, now turned yellow, lit up the forest. Cat brier, though an obstacle, was not insurmountable, and when I had to, I plunged through it at the cost of a few scratches.

But bull brier, a larger and fiercer relative of cat brier that grows prominently in some sunlit parts of the forest, was another story. Its fearsome, black-berried vines, less than a quarter of an inch in diameter, are as strong as leather thongs and bear large, needle-sharp, curving thorns. After one futile attempt, I did not challenge any more bull-brier thickets; they defy anyone not armed with a machete.

Where bull brier, like poison ivy, grows as high as the trees do, the Sunken Forest is virtually impenetrable. Luckily for me, the savage shoots of bull brier do not grow very high where the trees crowd in tightly overhead and shade it out. Some trees are festooned with strands of dead bull brier that are thorny enough but so weak and brittle that they can be pushed aside safely.

POISON IVY EMBRACING HOLLY

A FALL-TINGED CAT-BRIER LEAF

A BULL-BRIER ENTANGLEMENT

Odd Little Ridges

Where the bull brier and other underbrush thinned out I was able to see a considerable distance through the trees, but even where the ground cover was dense it was obvious that the forest floor was not as level as my first view of the fairly even treetops had suggested. In fact, the ground is broken by small, often steep ridges 10 to 15 feet high with valleys between them. These odd little ridges are actually dunes that were formed long ago and in the usual manner by wind-blown sand accumulating among clumps of beach grass. As Fire Island's beach grew wider over the years, the wind and the grass built successive new lines of dunes in front of existing lines, at intervals of perhaps a century. Gradually the dunes farthest from the sea were seeded and stabilized by vegetation and became the ridges seen in the Sunken Forest. If these ridges were stripped of their living cover, they would quickly revert to their dunelike look. That has been the fate of most of the rest of Fire Island and of many similar islands along the Atlantic coast where woodcutters, fire and cattle destroyed the vegetation.

The low swampy places among the ridges supported a different vegeta-

NEW GROWTH SPRINGING FROM A FALLEN RED MAPLE

tion from that of higher ground. Trees like hollies, sassafras and oaks will grow with their roots in saturated soil, and some were even thriving here. But red maples are even more tolerant of wet ground; many of the boggy spots were bordered by their light gray trunks. Although most of these maples grew straight and free, I saw one small bog, perhaps 60 feet across, where three large, healthy maples grew in the strangest of manners—toppled on their sides. Some of their many branches were embedded deep in the bog and half of their buttressed roots were high in the air.

How could the maples have survived—and even transcended—this uprooting? The explanation may be fairly simple. When the maples started growing a century or more ago, the bog was open and sunny. The maples grew toward light at the bog's center, rather than developing toward its boundaries, where they would have met the competition of trees that thrive on drier land. Maple limbs extending inward above the bog eventually grew so long and thick that—perhaps with some help from the hurricane of 1938—they unbalanced and uprooted the three trees. Not at all inconvenienced by this situation, the maples sent up new vertical trunks and shoots with leafy branches that triumphantly drank up the sunlight and occupied all the space above the little bog. So dense had they become when I saw them that scant sunlight reached the bog. Except for small feathery cinnamon ferns and patches of sphagnum moss, little grows there.

GREAT REEDS AND RED GLASSWORT IN THE SALT MARSH

I emerged from the forest on its northern edge, bordering the shallow waters of Great South Bay. Leaving the woods by my self-chosen route through a thick tangle of bushes was even more difficult than my approach to it had been. As the woods descended toward bay level and the leafy canopy began to open, the undergrowth became just as snarled as it had been on the ocean side. In addition, the ground underfoot was itself an obstacle—not firm sand but mostly soft organic ooze similar to the mud I had encountered in some of the forest's valleys.

On my first attempt to reach the bay, I was repulsed ignominiously, my head and shoulders entangled in briers, my feet sinking deep in the mud. I tried several times before I located a place where the footing was firm enough for me to advance a little farther. When at last I conquered the bush-and-mud barrier, I found myself on level ground, dotted here and there with milkweed in woolly bloom, at the edge of a small marsh.

Much of the marsh was covered with *Phragmites,* a tall grass commonly called great reed, with a graceful, feathery seed plume, and *Salicornia,* often called samphire or glasswort. This is a curious low plant with vertical stems of many branches that look like long green caterpillars. They are tender but brittle and filled with salty sap. Though some seashore people use them for salads or pickles, I have never developed a taste for them. But I did admire the intense blaze of orange or crimson that the Fire Island variety of *Salicornia* showed at this time of year.

A WOOLLY MILKWEED BLOSSOM

Also on the resilient turf of the marsh there were occasional patches of *Spartina patens,* a neat thin-bladed grass that I had seen in many other salt marshes. I was surprised to find it here. *Spartina* usually grows in marshes where the rising tide of the sea penetrates and periodically covers the grass with fresh salt water. But Great South Bay, largely separated from the ocean by the bulk of Fire Island, has only a distant connection with the ocean; since its tides are therefore slight, it is not as salt as the sea itself.

A Stubborn Holdout

As a consequence, the *Spartina* I found was handicapped, fighting a losing battle with *Phragmites* and other plants that threaten to choke it out because they are at home in brackish water. *Phragmites* is particularly suited to the mixture of sea and fresh water, and solidly occupies most of the bay shore of the Sunken Forest. But where I stood the *Spartina patens* was stubbornly holding out. Perhaps it was attracted

SPARTINA MARSH GRASSES

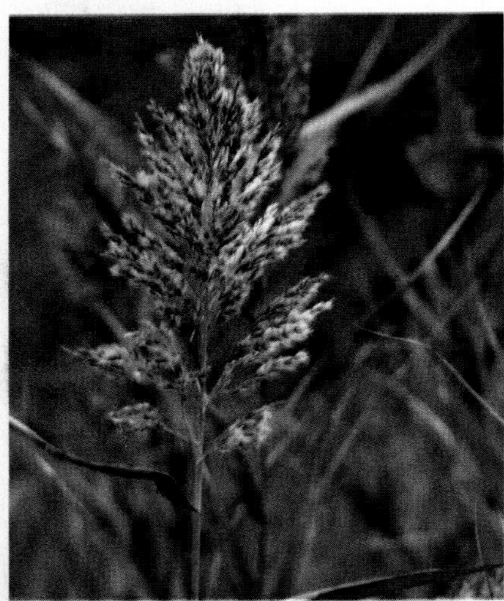

FLOWER OF A PHRAGMITES REED

in some way by the *Salicornia* growing near it—a plant *Spartina* frequently associates with on the edges of less hostile salt marshes.

A Windrow of Eelgrass

Beyond the salt marsh I came to a sandy beach a few feet wide where the small waves of Great South Bay were breaking with feeble pulses. At some recent time the waves here must have been somewhat stronger, for they had thrown up a continuous windrow of dead eelgrass, a green ribbonlike plant that grows submerged in the bay—and that I was glad to see. About 40 years ago the eelgrass along the Middle Atlantic coast was almost exterminated by a bacterial or fungus disease—scientists are not sure which. The plague drastically reduced the numbers of many water creatures that ate eelgrass or lived in its shelter, including the delicious bay scallops. Now eelgrass is making a comeback, and so are the scallops. I was equally pleased to find a lot of their fluted shells on the bay side of Fire Island.

A short way along the narrow beach I could see a branch of the Park Service path. I had in mind to return to the ocean side of the forest, and if I had used this path I would have been saved considerable exertion. But I was determined to go back through a part of the forest I had not yet seen. So I turned, crossed the little salt marsh with its brave *Spartina* and feathery *Phragmites* reeds and fought through the snarl of underbrush into the trees beyond. I was wiser now to the ways of the forest. I climbed over the ridges that were once white sand dunes, avoiding the bogs that lay in depressions between them, and skirted the bull brier.

It was more familiar territory now, and I was able to observe something about the trees that had escaped me before. The oaks and maples, which do not tolerate salt, grew farthest away from the ocean. Somewhat nearer the sea were the hollies, pitch pines and sassafras and the monstrous vines of poison ivy. Where the forest thinned on its beach side, the tangle of sturdy beach plum and bayberry reappeared. Finally came the open air with bearberry and beach grass underfoot.

Sweating and scratched, I turned my back to the cool salt breeze and looked once more at the forest. Even knowing that New York City was barely 50 miles away over the horizon to the west, it was not terribly difficult to imagine myself the first human being ever to make the journey I had just completed.

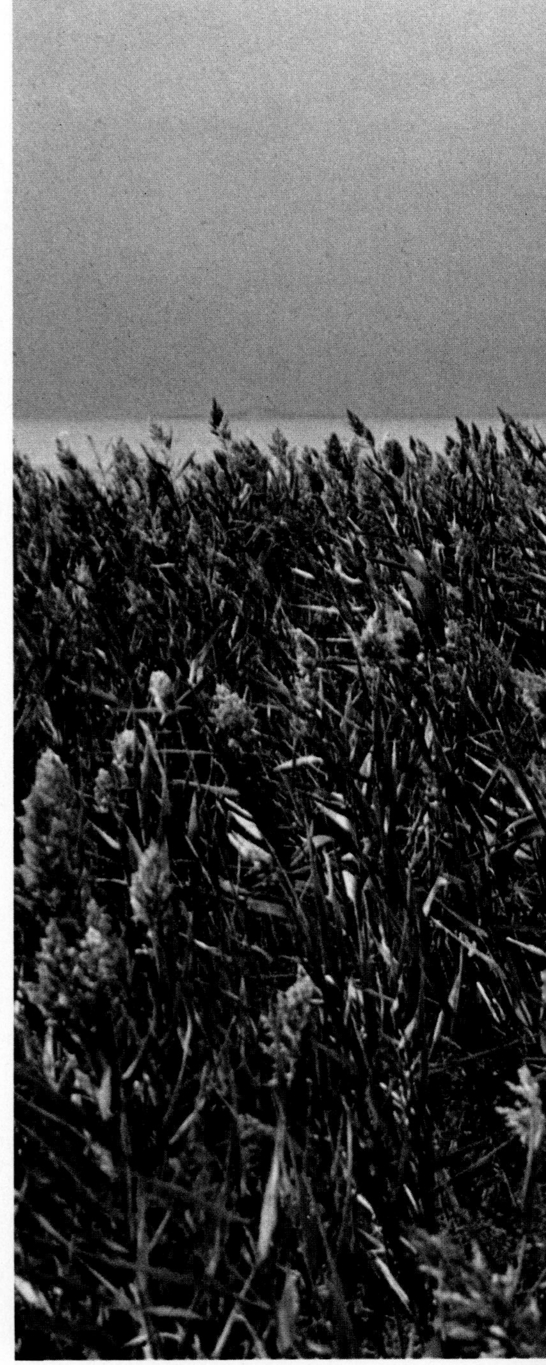

FEATHERY PHRAGMITES BORDERING GREAT SOUTH BAY

3/ The Living Beach

Sound of surf in these autumnal dunes — the continuousness of it, sound of endless charging, endless incoming and gathering, endless fulfilment and dissolution, endless fecundity, and endless death. HENRY BESTON/ *THE OUTERMOST HOUSE*

One of the delights of unfrequented beaches is the great variety of living things that can be seen along them. The sea itself is less revealing. It may be crowded with fish and other subsurface creatures, but people in a boat seldom see anything except perhaps some floating jellyfish. Forests are hardly better. Many a Boy Scout has tramped hopefully through miles of woods and spotted nothing but a few birds and a couple of squirrels. The forest may be full of other inhabitants but they are hidden by foliage or holed up for the day.

Beaches are wide open. You can see for miles along them and often for a good distance inland. Just beyond the water's edge lies the most thickly inhabited zone of the ocean, the teeming littoral, whose tight population pressure has sent beach fleas, hermit crabs, burrowing worms and all sorts of other interesting creatures pioneering up the beach between the levels of high and low tides. When the water surface is fairly smooth, schools of minnows and other tiny fish cruise in the shallows where they are relatively safe from bigger fish. Sometimes a big fish—a striped bass or a bluefish—can be glimpsed a bit farther out, or a shower of little fish jumping out of water shows where a hungry monster has dashed among them with gaping jaws.

For all its seeming emptiness, the open beach is nature's cafeteria, continuously decked with food supplied by sea and land. The supply is best when the wind is onshore. Then every wave carries its gift of edibles: crabs no larger than a pea, minute clams, an occasional dead fish or squid, bits of seaweed, pieces of wood with barnacles clinging to them. All these delicacies the wave deposits at its swash mark. If the tide is rising, the next wave carries them higher up the beach to form a concentration at high-water line. When the tide is falling, a thin tracery of provisions follows the swash marks of the retreating waves.

These offerings of food noticeably preoccupy the inhabitants of the beach. Most conspicuous are the long-legged shore birds like the plovers, sandpipers and snipe, which prefer their food fresh or just as the waves deposit it. Some of them patrol the water's edge on long, easy wings, alighting when they spot anything interesting that may prove edible. Others run along the sand, sometimes in shallow foaming water, taking to the air only when an extrastrong wave threatens them with a ducking. The smallest shore birds, the sandpipers, or "peeps," seem to prefer the swash marks of an ebbing tide. On walks, I have often enjoyed watching these sparrow-sized birds running along the beach, their tiny legs a blur as they try to keep safely ahead of me, but it took me quite a while to notice that they were not running in a straight line. In a very practical way they were following the scalloped curves of the swash marks, stopping for an instant now and then to snatch some morsel invisible to me.

Supplementing the delicacies delivered by the sea are those contributed by the land. In summer a considerable part of the food along the beach consists of swarms of hapless land insects that flew or were blown out to sea, fell into the water when they tired, then were washed ashore. On a Long Island beach I once found an enormous green-bronze beetle. It was fat, two inches long, with powerful pincers in front. I doubt that it was a native New Yorker. Perhaps it lost its bearings and flew for many miles from some southerly land before the ocean finally claimed it and washed it up. When I first saw the beetle, two black-bellied plovers were pecking tentatively at its glittering armor, trying to get at the treasure trove of exotic food inside it.

In spring an occasional contribution of the land to the commissary of the beach seems to be black ants, particularly the winged males and females that set out to form new colonies. Several times I have found a series of swash marks outlined in the solid black of massed dead ants. For half an hour or so I waited near one such place to see how the shore birds would take to this food. Some snipe inspected the ants, rejected them and departed. Then came a dozen little peeps. They tasted the ants, found them acceptable and ate and ate.

Shown magnified eight times, a beach flea browses in the sand near the water. If disturbed, it can leap several feet in any direction.

At night the wilder beaches are patrolled by animals that live some distance inland. These are mostly skunks and raccoons, but foxes sometimes join them. A long-beamed flashlight will sometimes catch them nibbling at a stranded fish, the raccoons holding their food daintily in black paws. When spotlighted, raccoons will run clumsily into the beach grass, but skunks will stare defiantly and saunter away, knowing well that they need fear no one. I have never seen a fox on a beach, but I have been told that when surprised they jump like coiled springs and vanish in a flash.

Although birds and land animals use the beach as a larder, they do not live permanently on wave-battered sand. To do this successfully demands special adaptation, for the strip between the high and low tide is a difficult environment. If there are large and numerous rocks at tide level, fascinating sea creatures, hundreds of different kinds, live happily among them. Barnacles and sea anemones resembling tentacled flowers colonize them; starfish and clusters of mussels cling to them among the seaweeds, and whelks shelter under the weeds and prey on the barnacles and shellfish.

But open, rockless beaches are another matter. The ones most hostile to life are pebble beaches exposed to the open ocean. Hardly anything can survive in the rattling mill of the pebbles, which are hard to burrow into and which grind against one another whenever a wave breaks. Not quite so hostile are exposed beaches of pure sand. Shellfish and marine worms that want to be safe from the violence of the waves can burrow down a foot or so when the tide brings the dangerous surf toward them, then come up again when the coast is clear. At low tide many sand beaches, especially those that do not get too hard a pounding from the open ocean, are full of holes showing that something is residing below. If the hole sends up a squirt of water when footsteps approach, it probably belongs to a clam. If it does not, it may be the home of a sea worm. The word "worm" suggests drabness, but some of these animals are remarkably colorful. The clam worm, a common inhabitant of clam beds, is an iridescent mixture of blue and green, touched with red in the tentacles, with orange bristlelike feet along its sides. These worms are a favorite bait of fishermen, but they can inflict a painful bite on an inexperienced handler; children and most parents should not try to dig a clam worm from its burrow.

A little higher up the beach the sand is too dry for clams or worms. Here is the chosen home of the beach fleas, those sand-colored shrimp-

On Cape Cod's Great Island a herring gull stands guard over her active brood of three chicks, newly hatched from spotted grayish-brown eggs. By far the most common species of sea bird along the Atlantic coast, herring gulls breed in the spring and usually make their nests at ground level on coastal islands. The fuzzy infants grow feathers rapidly and take to the air in about six weeks. But they do not become fully mature until they are about four years old —having by then lived approximately one third of the normal gull life span.

like hopping creatures with pale-blue crossed eyes. They burrow deep into the sand to avoid the threat of the rising tide, then come up to forage on the surface when the waves have retreated. I suppose they must be considered sea creatures since they apparently require salty dampness; they are never far from wet sand, but they have taken the first steps toward life on dry land. Perhaps a few million years from now their descendants may learn to live in the beach grass and never approach the beach itself except at night when the tide is out.

The engaging little ghost crabs of the more southerly Atlantic beaches have progressed further in this critical transition. They are almost land animals, and have solved the problem of making a living on a wave-pounded beach by moving to its upper reaches and digging their burrows there. But they, too, have maintained ties with the sea. There the female crab lays her eggs and there the larvae live until instinct urges them toward the beach. Here they dig a hole to shelter themselves until they assume the shape of their parents. As growing crabs, they move ever higher on the beach, progressing from a burrow dampened by the incoming tide to one above the high-tide mark and, finally, as full-grown crabs, to homes in the beach grass. Even there, however, they are indebted to the ocean. The ghost crab has not yet evolved into a creature that can breathe in open air; it must get its oxygen from water. And so periodically it bathes in the swash of a wave, where it half fills a small chamber that is part of its gill system. From this supply, which it replenishes a few times a day, it draws the necessary oxygen by diffusion through the membranes of its gills.

I had heard about these crabs but had never seen them until I visited the Virginia end of the national seashore on Assateague Island. On a darkly threatening day I was riding in a truck with a Park Service ranger on a remote part of the beach when he slowed down and pointed. "Ghost crabs," he said. "They don't think trucks are dangerous." Close to the ruts were two fragile-looking crabs about three inches across their folded legs. Except for dark eyes held up on stalks like periscopes, they were almost exactly the color of the sand. They were confronting each other with open claws. The ranger stopped the truck near them. "They're fighting or mating or something. They come out on dark days like this one when they think the gulls aren't around. Try stepping out of the truck and see what happens." I got out of the truck 10 feet from the crabs, but when I looked for them they had vanished. "That's why they're called ghost crabs," said the ranger. "They're magic."

Late that afternoon I walked alone along a deserted part of the beach carrying a flashlight and a picnic supper in a haversack. While the sun was still up, I saw no crabs at all. They might not be afraid of trucks, but their tiny brains were accurately programed to make them hide from human beings. Their lacy tracks and the entrances to their burrows were everywhere, small holes on the middle beach near high-water mark, larger holes farther back among the clumps of beach grass. About the time the sun went down, I saw a very small crab scuttle across the sand and disappear into a hole. "Reckless juvenile," I thought. Gulls were still cruising along the beach, and I myself, no doubt, looked like a peril to crab life.

Not long after sundown I found a thriving stretch of beach grass with many large crab holes among the green clumps. This, I decided, was a high-class residential district where large, successful crabs had set up their establishments at a safe distance from the dangerous beach. I sat down among the holes, which were perhaps 1 1/2 inches in diameter and three or four feet apart, ate my sandwiches and waited while the darkness gathered. Nothing happened for a time. Then, in the failing light, I saw a large crab sitting quietly on the threshold of the nearest hole, watching me with its periscope eyes. I tried to sit perfectly still but must have made some slight motion, for after a moment the crab vanished, presumably down its hole. It did not reappear, but soon other crabs were sitting on their thresholds. It was quite dark by this time, and I wondered why these senior citizens of the beach still stayed so close to home. Then I saw a single gull soaring above the water's edge. It dived sharply, hopped a couple of times and made swallowing motions with its beak and neck. Late bird had got early crab.

The prudent inhabitants of the better residential area waited 20 minutes more until all the gulls had retired for the night. Then they scuttled off sideways for a feast of their own, on morsels of dead fish and bits of seaweed. I played the flashlight around and found the sand alive with big and little crabs.

At night the beach of Assateague belongs to the ghost crabs. Their worst enemies are sea birds, and most of these are diurnal creatures. Nocturnal herons apparently do not prey on the crabs, and I am sure no ground animal such as a skunk or fox is quick enough to catch them. Ghost crabs can run amazingly fast: they can run forward or backward, and when they zigzag they can move like lightning. They do this by running sideways and changing their leading edge without stopping —as much to even the work load on their legs as to take evasive action.

Startled by a flashlight, a night-feeding ghost crab freezes in its tracks at the water's edge. Hunger is not the only reason these pale, small crustaceans come to the ocean from their burrows in the dry upper beach. Though well adapted to life on land, the ghost crab, a gill-breathing marine species, must return to the sea several times a day to replenish the supply of water in the internal chambers surrounding its gills.

In darkness they feel so secure that they do not run away when a man approaches, and they do not know what to make of a flashlight beam. Caught in a spot of light, a ghost crab stands perfectly still except for its periscope eyes, which swing in bewilderment. Its brain works slowly to solve the novel problem, but when it reaches a conclusion its action is instantaneous. The crab simply vanishes. I worked this trick a dozen times, holding the crab in a circle of light about a foot across. One instant the crab was there, the next instant it was gone. I decided that the effectiveness of this disappearing act depends on the crab's protective coloration and speed of movement. Before the human eye or brain can decide which way to turn the beam, the creature is out of the spot of light and far away in the darkness.

Though they must visit the edge of the sea to wet their gills, ghost crabs seem wary of the water, and with reason: if one of them is surprised by the swash of a wave, it is in danger of being rolled along as helplessly as a frond of seaweed. If it is unlucky enough to be caught in the surf, it will try to reach the bottom and stay there until the wave subsides. Only the young crabs seem to get caught; the bigger and wiser ones are evidently more alert. All of them appear to find plenty to eat at the sea's table. Generally they are found sitting with their front pair of claws held to their mouths, chewing contentedly on some delicious tidbit that the friendly tide has brought to their beach.

Herring gulls, the ghost crabs' nemesis, also find plenty to eat on the beach. The tide is as friendly to gulls as it is to crabs. Once on a New Jersey beach I saw a great flock of herring gulls working on a mass of large hard-shell clams stranded by the tide. There were so many clams that they made a solid band several feet wide and a hundred yards long. Most of them were still alive and holding their shells tight shut, but the gulls were carrying them up in the air and dropping them on the other clams to smash them open. It may have been my imagination, but those gulls seemed to me to be flying more heavily than usual, their stomachs stuffed. Only their voracious greed kept them feeding.

Herring gulls, fierce but graceful, with immaculate coats of smooth gray and white, are the most familiar birds along Eastern beaches. For all their attractive looks and meticulous grooming they are largely scavengers whose natural way of life is not to catch herrings but to cruise the beaches picking up anything edible that comes ashore, mostly dead fish. Another important source of food is shellfish, principally clams or mussels, which the gulls drop on rocks or any convenient hard surface

in order to break the shells. They generally drop these from 20 or 30 feet up and follow down in a power swoop to keep other gulls from stealing the shattered morsels. On rockless beaches this tactic is less effective, so a gull picks up the same clam repeatedly and drops it on the soft sand. The shell is not broken, but the clam becomes fatigued by the successive shocks and allows the gull to pry it open. When a new blacktop road or parking lot is built near a mussel bed, the gulls instantly discover the new smashing surface and litter it with the broken blue shells of the mussels.

A generation or two ago the beaches supported a moderate army of scavenging herring gulls but nothing like the hordes that thrive today. The mainstay of the present gull population is garbage—thrown on dumps where flocks of gulls, screaming their wild cries, fight over anything that is edible.

Until recently I wondered fruitlessly where dump gulls spend the night. They do not stay at the dumps, as I had determined by checking my hometown's dump on Cape Cod. Some bird experts told me the gulls go to the beaches after sundown, but on my walks I did not see sufficient numbers of them there to bear this out.

I cleared up the mystery in a very simple manner—as far as the local gulls are concerned. One summer morning I awoke at 5 o'clock. An open window near my bed faced the seashore about half a mile away, beyond a built-up area and some salt marshes. Through the window came a curious sound, a high-pitched cry, or the merging of many cries. "Gulls," I thought. "Thousands of them." I listened while the sound waxed and waned. After half an hour or so it died away.

Next morning I got up at 4, drove to the edge of the salt marsh and followed a plank walk across it that led to the back of the beach. It was still dark; only a few sleepy gull cries came from across a broad creek. I sat down and waited, staring into the darkness. Files of night herons (called quawks by Cape Codders) flapped slowly past, voicing their dismal croaks. A few small birds flitted about like bats.

Then came the first dawn in the east, and the cries across the creek began to gather volume. Hundreds of gulls spoke in chorus using all the words of their vocabulary: the harsh scream, the twanging mew, the gentle mutter, the clucking. As the light grew brighter I began to see them: faint dark dots on the water of the creek, ranks of lighter dots against the marsh beyond. There were many hundreds of them, possibly thousands. These were the gulls that got their living at the town dumps. This was their home, and this their social hour.

I climbed to the top of a nearby dune to watch them better as the sun rose. From this vantage point I could see that most of the gulls were sitting on an island of ground slightly higher than the surrounding marsh. It had a few bushes on it, mostly bayberry, which proved that it was not often covered by high tide. The birds sat close in congenial ranks, showing none of the fierce combativeness of their daytime hours. Small flocks of them would take off, fly in a circle and land again, or hover for a few moments above their fellows. Waves of sound swept the colony. At times it seemed all the gulls were screaming; then would come a pause of near silence, the kind that sometimes descends on gatherings of chattering humans.

When the sun rose above the mist on the eastern horizon, the gulls' socializing ended. Flocks of 50 to 100 rose from the ground and flew off purposefully, headed for their favorite dumps. In half an hour the entire host was gone except for a few conservative birds that preferred to scavenge along the shore in the ancestral way. As I walked back across the marsh I reflected that most evils have something in their favor. If it were not for those reeking dumps, I probably would never have seen that mighty company of Cape Cod gulls enjoying their social hour on the salt marsh of my hometown.

As far as beaches are concerned, there is one evil that is unalloyed: the motor vehicle. To enjoy a beach to the full you should use your own two feet. It is best to wear shoes, preferably comfortable work or sport shoes with thick soles. They do not sink into the sand as much as flexible bare feet, and thus save energy. Do not walk at the pace of a competitive hiker. If you do, your feet will dig in at every step, and you will tire in half the time that you would if you were walking on hard ground. Walk slowly. You will see more and enjoy more. You are not going anywhere anyway.

One of the best times to walk on a beach is when the tide is going out or is at full ebb, and the best place is near the water. The birds are busier there, and you stand a good chance of finding jellyfish, seaweed encrusted with the coiled tubes of tiny marine worms, and other things, less commonly seen, that have just drifted ashore and are still alive or were recently. On a Virginia beach, I once found at the water's edge a 10-foot timber one side of which was covered with barnacles—not the familiar acorn barnacles that cling to rocks and pilings but the variety known as goosenecks, with fleshy stalks tipped by what look like two small clamshells. The barnacles were still alive. While the timber

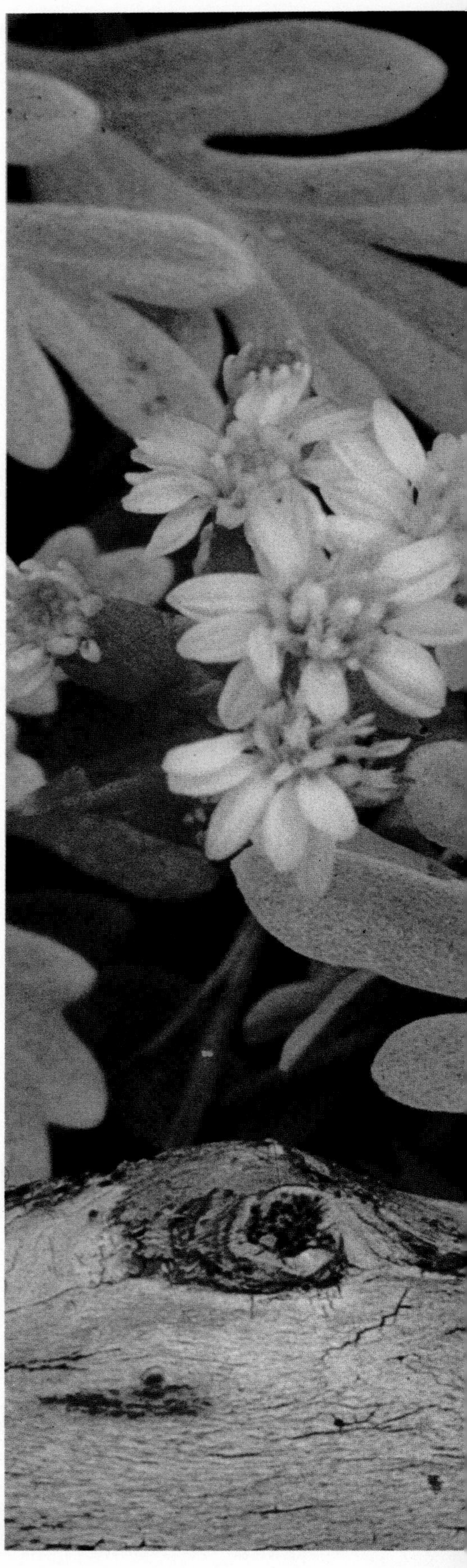

rocked in the gentle breakers, they opened their "shells" and combed the water with food-gathering tentacles. Their stalks had grown three inches long, which meant that the timber—their world—had floated for months or even years in salt water. Now the barnacles were in danger of dying, from being either eaten by gulls or stranded by the tide and left to dry out. I pushed the timber into the sea. A slight breeze was blowing offshore, and this, perhaps combined with a local current, made the wood float farther away. I hoped that the Gulf Stream would pick it up and send it and its inhabitants on a pleasant voyage to Europe.

Usually beyond any attempt at salvation are the beautiful crested jellyfish known as the Portuguese men-of-war that are sometimes found dying on beaches as far from their native tropics as Cape Cod. Kept afloat by their blue and pink saillike crests, which are filled with a buoyant gas, they are carried northward by the Gulf Stream and cast ashore by an unlucky wind or current. Their many tentacles—as long as 50 feet in a large Portuguese man-of-war—trail across the sand, and even though the creature may have been dead for hours the tentacles, armed with cells to poison and paralyze prey, can still inflict a painful sting.

I have taken some of my most fruitful walks on a beach during the extralow tides that come immediately after a new or full moon. Then the offshore bars are well out of water, and the pools behind them are protected from the waves. Schools of tiny fish—mostly the young of larger fish—shelter in the shallows, skittering this way or that at the slightest alarm. Sometimes pale cigar-shaped squid hunt them there. The squid cruises with its pinkish-gray tentacles held forward together, pushed along by its jet-propulsion system, taking in water through its outer covering and forcing it out through a funnel near the head that can be pointed in any direction. When the color of the bottom changes, the squid's color changes to match; for instance, when it passes over a belt of pebbles it can turn brown by expanding pigment cells on its body surface. In one tidal pool I found a textbook example of biological cooperation that I had up to then only read about: a hermit crab, its soft rear end tucked into a coiled snail shell, with a sea anemone riding on top and waving its tentacles. The shell protects the crab's tender hinder parts; the anemone gets carried to good feeding places, and its stinging tentacles frighten away common enemies. The crab was, I thought, very pleased with itself.

The crab had probably searched long and diligently before it found the shell that now housed it comfortably. Just any shell will not suit a

A dusty miller owes its powdered look to white hairs that retard the evaporation of moisture.

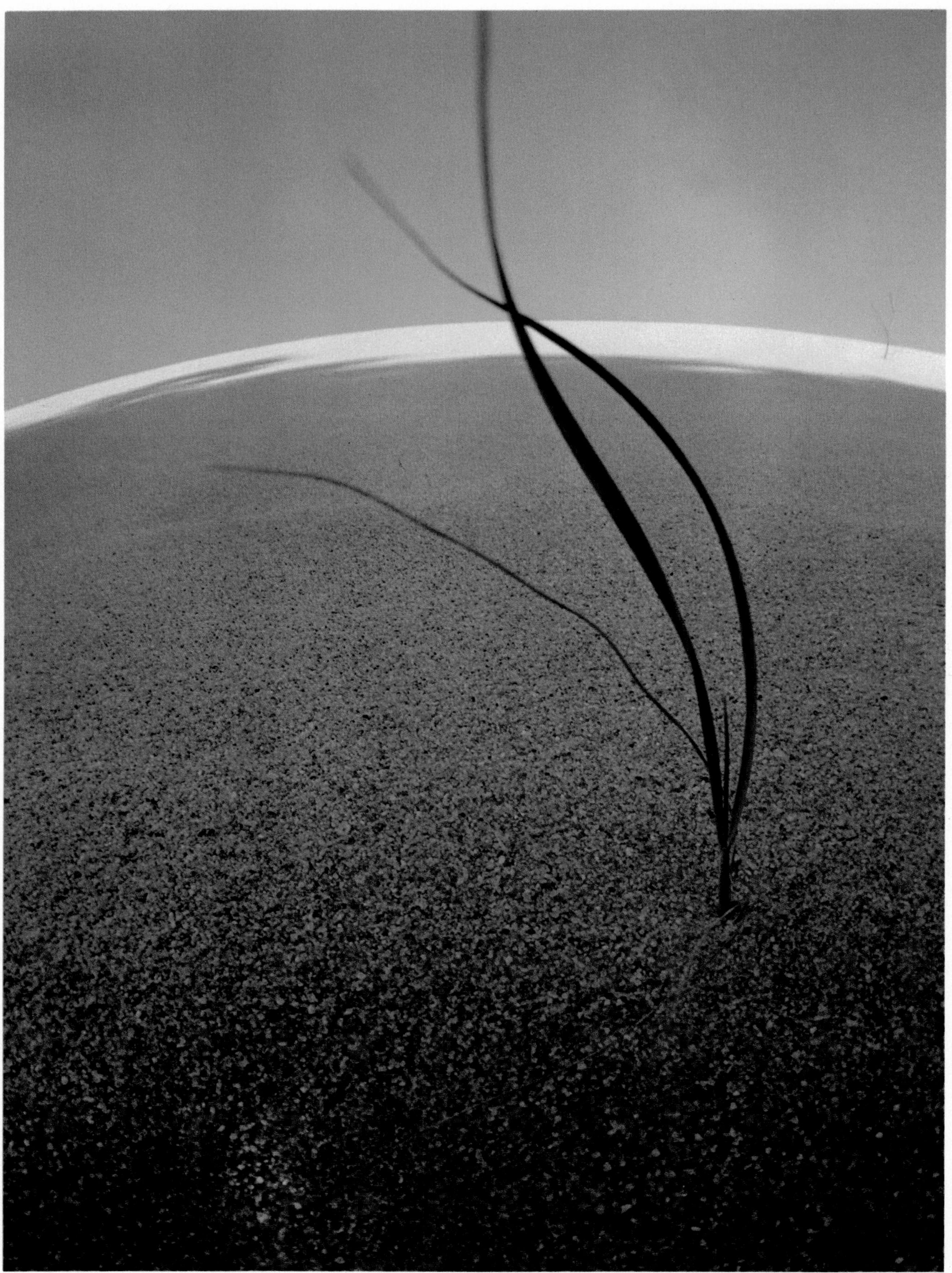

Pioneering a bare dune, slim spears of beach grass branch from a network of roots that helps anchor the shifting sands.

hermit crab, which must switch domiciles constantly as its body grows larger. Only certain kinds of snail shells have spirals that correspond properly to the curves of the crab's soft parts, and not all such shells will do. When it comes time for househunting, the crab may carefully investigate a number of potential shelters, rolling them over with its claws and examining them for soundness, reaching into them to make sure they are unoccupied and finally backing into them to try them on for size. If a shell does not pass all the tests, the crab pops back into the protection of its old house and continues to search until satisfied.

The best time for finding sea shells and similar delicate treasures cast ashore by the sea is when the tide is out. Many of the shells found on a beach are left there by crustaceans—particularly crabs—that have molted in the process of growing. Since molting is a cyclical event that occurs to groups of crabs in a particular generation, you will often run across molted shells in considerable concentrations. Most other shells belong to creatures that normally live safely below the level of low tide. Perhaps a few of them were pushed higher up by population pressure; perhaps they were merely reckless. In either case they ventured too far; the suction of a wave caught them and threw them up on the beach. Sometimes large numbers of a single species are cast up by a storm. During a recent stroll on one of my favorite beaches—Sandy Neck on the inner curve of Cape Cod—I picked up an unusually large assortment of interesting items. Among them were sand collars: the eggs of the large moon snail cemented together with sand to form a round, collar-shaped object. The "collar" is translucent: held up to the sunlight, it reveals the hundreds of eggs within. Another snail, the knobbed whelk, deposits its eggs in a chain of disk-shaped capsules, also translucent, which are held together at the edge. Sometimes the capsules are empty; sometimes they are full of the tiny white coiled shells of baby snails that did not have time to emerge from their shelter before it was thrown up on the beach.

The snails whose eggs I found belong to the endlessly varied mollusk clan, but the beach also held traces of another enormous group of marine dwellers, the echinoderms. These creatures are distinctive in being radially symmetrical—they have no true front or back—and typically they are covered with hundreds of spines. But their most interesting feature—absent in only a few species of echinoderms—is that their bodies are assembled from parts that come in fives or multiples of five. Here and there I saw the thin, white, disk-shaped skeletons of sand dollars, each with a five-petaled "flower" engraved on its top; I also found brown sand dollars that were still alive and could still crawl slowly by moving their tiny spines when I placed them on sand under water. Another find, closely related to the sand dollar, was the Cape Cod variety of sea urchin, a brownish-green ball covered with short, inoffensive spines; when it dies the spines fall off, leaving a green empty shell that resembles a round cushion with five segments sewed together. The northern starfish I picked up, also echinoderms in good standing, each displayed the identifying five arms. Each arm was grooved on the underside, the groove lined with the tiny sucker-equipped tubular feet by which a starfish moves.

On another walk I took on Sandy Neck, I noted that a heavy surf the previous night had littered the sand not only with dead and dying creatures but with seaweed torn from the sea bottom by the waves. There was frilly greenish Irish moss, which, when fresh, can be taken home, boiled and eaten as a jellylike pudding with milk, sugar and vanilla. (I find its bland, sea-tinged flavor delicious, but my wife cannot abide it.) There was a kind of kelp made up of long, rubbery, ruffled blades, most of them still attached to stones by rootlike holdfasts. These castaways had been unlucky enough to put their trust in stones too small to withstand the pull of the waves.

The commonest seaweeds along that beach are sea lettuce, which is bright green and looks like lettuce but has a rubbery texture, and brown rockweed of several species that clings to rocks and keeps itself upright in the water by means of little oval gas-filled floats at the ends of its branches. When the waves are especially high they dislodge another weed, *Codium,* which resembles a many-branched candelabra, and whose fronds are round and feel like a sponge. Along with these plants are real sponges: small, gray, humble animals with fingerlike branches too small and hard to be of any use as bath sponges.

When I had walked for a while along the water's edge, I crossed the beach to high-water mark, where the highest tides and waves of recent weeks had swept up and concentrated in one tangled line everything loose that they had found on the beach. A few feet behind this mark the beach vegetation began. The nearest to the beach, and thus the most exposed to risk, were annual plants—ground-hugging seaside spurge, fleshy-leaved sandwort and sea rocket, whose seeds are carried by the sea itself and washed far up the beach by the highest waves. In spring I have seen lines of little sea-rocket seedlings following the scalloped curves of the swash marks. Their best chance for survival is the fact that the normally milder waves of summer will not reach them. Those that try to grow too far down on the beach risk dousing with sea water and do not thrive.

Just behind these long-shot gamblers begins the beach grass, that wonderful, heroic plant that creates the sand dunes and with them much of the beauty of the beach. When a beach is healthy—that is, when its sand is not blowing or washing away and not too many people are trampling on it—the graceful fountains of grass sweep toward the sea in a gently sloping apron. The clumps spread by means of underground runners, each producing many smaller clumps by the end of summer. Where the grass is thick, the sand among the clumps usually stands several inches higher than it does in the open a few feet away. This means that the grass is catching fresh sand. Next spring it will grow higher and catch more sand. Perhaps a high new dune will rise at that point. Or perhaps storm waves will wash it back to the line of the older dunes. The beach grass will never stop trying to advance the dune line seaward.

At least it will not stop trying if it is not handicapped by some outside influence. If the beach is deprived of sand by a jetty or a breakwater, it will become narrower. The waves will not break as far out; they will surge higher up the beach, undermining the established dunes and turning them into steep, concave sand cliffs instead of gentle, grass-covered slopes.

Equally bad for the grass is "people erosion." Beach grass cannot stand trampling. It grows in sand so loose that human feet dig down and disturb the tender roots. A few pairs of feet per day climbing up a slope covered with beach grass can kill many of its clumps. Soon a bare path forms; the wind blasts through it and excavates a notch. If people walk through the notch, as they are likely to do, they may wear it down to beach level in a single season. Beach vehicles are even worse. A single passage by one of them may do damage that nature cannot repair for years.

If the dune created by the beach grass survives the attacks of storm waves and other hazards, it is gradually colonized by additional hardy plants that can grow with their roots in pure sand and their tops in salty spray. One of the hardiest is the lovely seaside goldenrod—much like its better-known inland cousin but furnished with fleshier leaves to help it conserve moisture. I have seen it thriving only a few feet behind the most venturesome clumps of beach grass. Another is the beach pea, a relative of the sweet pea, which spreads by underground stems and decorates the summer sand with violet flowers.

Two foreign immigrants are welcome invaders of Atlantic beaches. Both are Asian in origin and both are former garden plants that escaped to live in a wild state. One, flaunting lovely spikes of golden flowers, is dusty miller. It is named for the powdery look of its leaves —covered with tiny hairs that are a moisture-saving adaptation to its salt-air habitat. The other is the salt-spray rose, a wild rose as beautiful as any highly bred variety, which seems to love hardship. On the shore near my hometown on Cape Cod it thrives on the foremost dunes. I know one plant that has grown in the course of years into a clump 40 feet in diameter; in spring it is covered with lovely pink flowers and later with scarlet rose hips. The storm waves burst in smothers of foam no more than 10 yards from it.

Just behind the foremost dunes a succession of woody plants begins. Beach plums, short and shrubby compared to their cultivated orchard cousins, thrive despite only meager protection against the wind. Their fruit, a delicacy appreciated by both birds and people—it is used to make jams and jellies—is most abundant when the plants grow on the landward slopes of the dunes. Poison ivy thrives there also, a fine erosion preventer; it holds the sand with its tangled vines and also keeps people away from vulnerable dunes it has colonized.

If a belt of sand dunes is more than 50 yards deep, the next zone is likely to be occupied by two low-growing, sand-loving plants: bearberry and beach heather, sometimes called poverty grass because it will grow in very poor soil. Bearberries are slender trailing vines that make a dense mat and in late summer are bright with woody red berries. Beach heather grows a few inches high in solid sheets or rounded clumps that cover themselves with small yellow flowers in June.

Often these two low-growers completely dominate the patches of sand that they occupy, not even permitting the hardy beach grass to trespass there. I suspect—though it's only a hunch—that the explanation of this botanical oddity may be that both bearberries and beach heather inject the soil with a material that hinders the growth of other plants. In any event, I have planted beach grass in bare sand between clumps of beach heather and watched it die in a season. Virtually the only plant that thrives in such places is gray-green reindeer moss, a many-branched lichen that—rootless like all lichens—merely sits on the soil between the clumps where the wind cannot blow it away.

Behind the beach-heather belt begins the world of dry land, with such plants as pine and oak, so I returned to walking along the sand —hundreds of yards from my starting point—to see what else I could find at high-water mark. The long windrow of flotsam had been there quite a while. Most of it was seaweed, dry and hard. There were some fish embedded in it, partly devoured by birds or animals; what remained was by now too dry to offend the nose. In this seaweed it is possible sometimes to find a fair-sized shark; if you are lucky enough to come upon one you can extract its savage teeth as gleaming white gifts that children will enjoy. Odd-shaped fish bones polished to ivory by wind and sand are worth collecting too, and so are "mermaid's purses," dark-brown, pillowlike objects with a tendril extending from each corner. They are the leathery egg cases of skates, broad, flat fish resembling sting rays. You may find kinds of sponge that you have not seen before, or shells entangled in the seaweed.

The last time I walked on Sandy Neck I found a boat shell, the single shell of a mollusk that clings to rocks. It is shaped like an inch-long oval boat and has a horizontal "seat" at one end. These shells are rare on the inner curve of Cape Cod, and I remember my joy when as a child I went to visit on the south side of the Cape and found a lot of them. They floated beautifully, just like boats, so I took a dozen of them home and fitted them with masts (grass stalks embedded in a drop of melted candle grease) threaded through sails made of squares of green leaf. When launched on still water they sailed reasonably well. Perhaps when I find a few more I shall demonstrate this art to relatives of mine who are children still.

Relics of an Unseen Life

PHOTOGRAPHS BY HARALD SUND

The beach is a place of opportunity and danger, of sudden death and quickening life. Here generations of creatures can find food in plenty, but only at the risk of providing meals for creatures swifter, larger or better armed than themselves.

This drama of survival takes place largely unseen by human eyes. Because beach animals live in a world that is constantly battered by the surf and threatened by predators, they tend to be wary; most species spend the daylight hours out of sight under the sand.

Yet the drama can be clearly detected in the remains that litter the beach surface. These relics—bits of clamshells, a beached angler fish, a leathery tangle of seaweed—lie strewn on the sand amid pebbles and driftwood in patterns that appear random but are in fact meaningful: they echo the beat of countless lives pursued not only on and under the sand but also in the sea itself.

The story begins offshore, where the microscopic plants and animals that are collectively known as plankton breed in billions. These floating organisms, along with larger marine creatures that feed upon them and one another, are washed ashore on every wave, and deposited at the wave's swash mark—the point at which it reaches the limit of its passage up the beach.

This deposit, or detritus, provides a rich bounty of food for the creatures of the strand, and they make the most of it. Much of the detritus is eaten off the surface by sea birds, crabs and other beach prowlers; clams extend necklike appendages that siphon plankton down from the surface to their underground habitats. But the clams themselves are hardly secure from harm; thrown up on the beach by churning wave action they may be seized, broken open and devoured by gulls—whose eggs and unwary chicks, in turn, may be eaten by other gulls or by raccoons and occasional foxes that patrol the beach borders.

For all the wastage, however, life is unremittingly handed from generation to generation. Indeed, under normal circumstances, the creatures of the beach community are enormously fecund. A crab, for example, can carry half a million eggs at one time, while an oyster can produce half a billion eggs in a single season; and even though few hatchlings survive predation long enough to reproduce, there are more than sufficient to perpetuate the species.

Feathers ruffled by the wind, a dead herring gull lies on a Cape Cod beach. A voracious predator in life, the gull will now provide food for other creatures—from insects to raccoons —before the tide sweeps it away.

The dark swash marks on the beach at left contain marine remains—small clams, beached fish, uprooted seaweed —dumped twice a day by the tides. The swash marks are carefully scavenged by shore birds such as sandpipers, plovers and turnstones.

Stranded by the ebbing tide, a tender fragment of algae, its furry tendrils half dried, stands out against surf-created sand ripples. As it decomposes, such a tidbit will not be ignored by the sand worms that live under the surface at the water's edge.

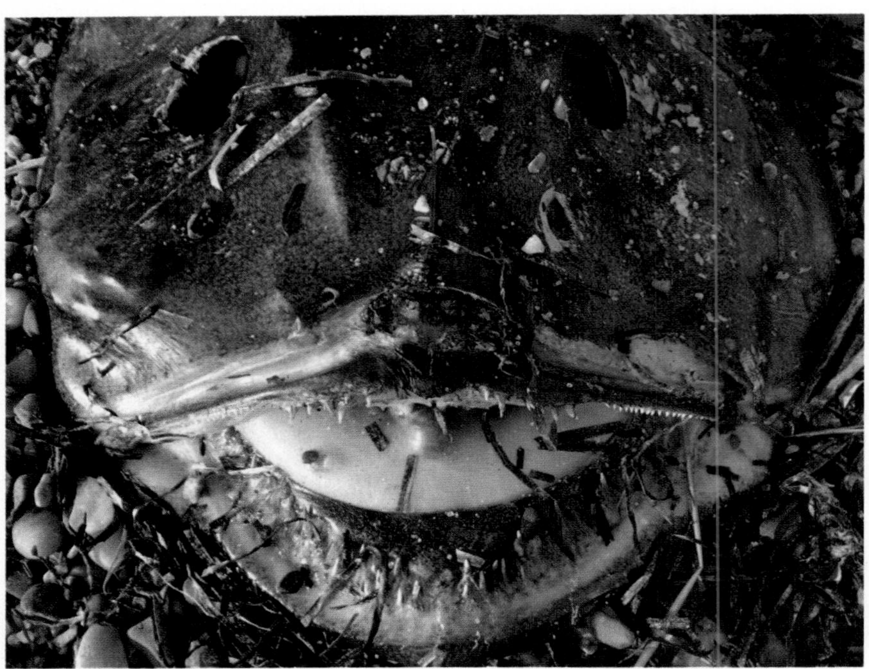
ANGLER FISH

SKATE'S EGG CASE

RAZOR CLAM

HORSESHOE-CRAB SHELL

Natural Artifacts of the Beach

Many of the larger beach remains —even the skeletal angler-fish head shown at top, far left—have the preserved look of artifacts unearthed in some archeological dig and mounted for display. But their resemblance to museum specimens is misleading: these varied relics represent the ongoing life-and-death struggle that the rigorous beach environment imposes on all its inhabitants.

Some of the shells are so beautiful that the functional efficiency of their design is overlooked. The slender bladelike shell of a razor clam enables it, digging with its long curving foot, to burrow down into the sand fast enough to escape a man clamming for his supper. But the same clam may be ambushed by a moon snail, whose passage through sand is speeded by the streamlined smoothness of its shell.

Not all beach relics, of course, are the litter of lost battles. The empty shell of a horseshoe crab is usually a sign of growth and survival; as it matures, this creature periodically outgrows and sheds its shell, then hides in the sand below low-water mark until its new shell hardens.

The flat, horny egg case of a skate may signify either the renewal of life or its end. If the skin is broken open, its contents may have escaped to survive as a new generation of skates. If the case is unopened, the embryonic skates inside are doomed —to be eaten by a gull or simply to dry up in their leathery envelope.

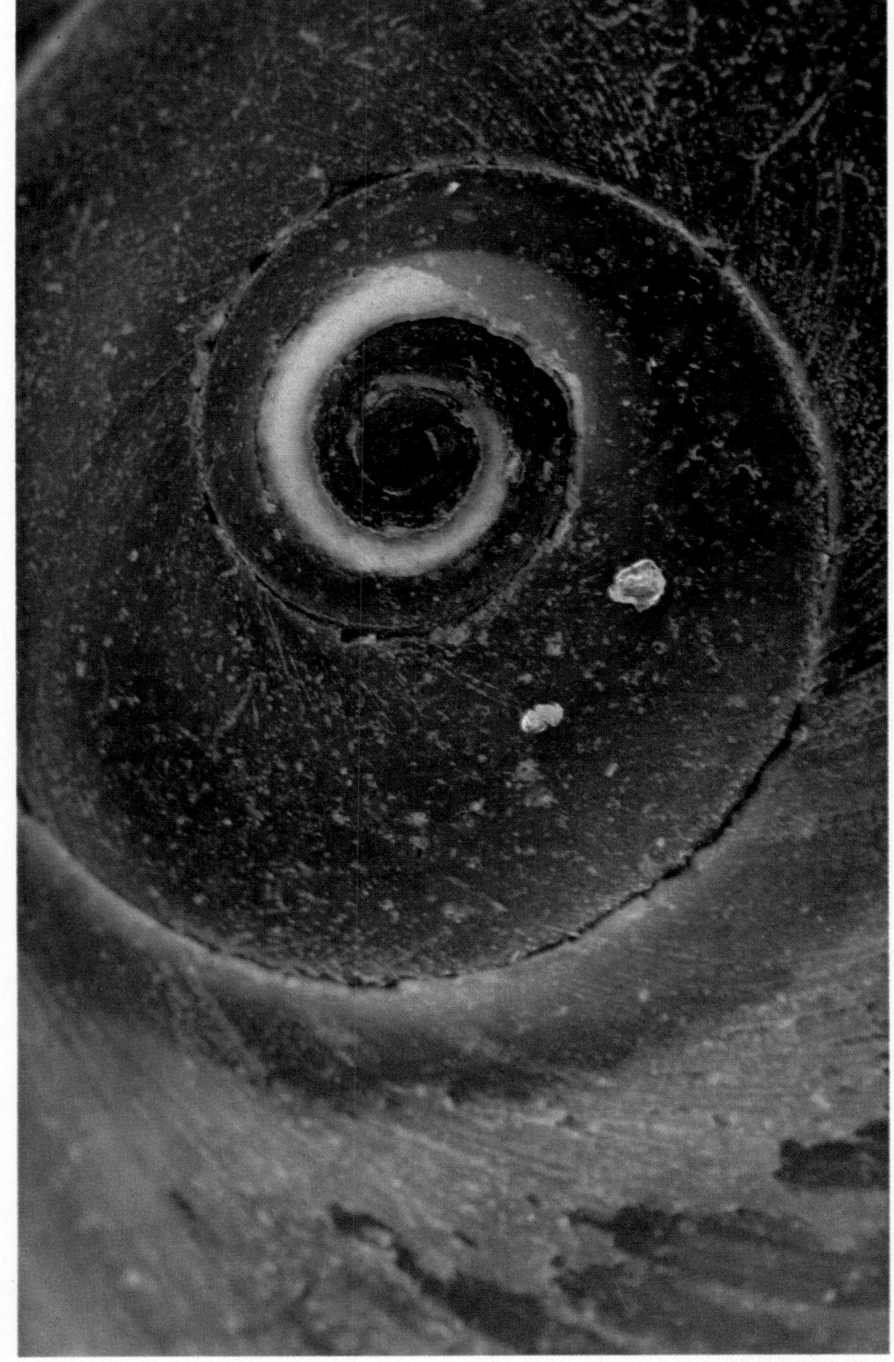

MOON-SNAIL SHELL

A seemingly useless bit of flotsam, this piece of driftwood and the seaweeds caught under it on a rocky Cape Cod beach are, though dead, rich with the promise of life. The speckled seaweed is eelgrass, favorite food of brant geese. The eelgrass ribbons and the log itself are coated—when washed ashore—with a thin film containing algae and protozoa, the basis of the food chain. Even the fragile gull feather will do its part as it decomposes; releasing its rich phosphates and protein, it will nourish such sand-growing plants as sea rocket, saltwort, cocklebur and spurge.

4/ Barriers and Bays

Now the great winds shorewards blow;/ Now the salt tides seawards flow;/ Now the wild white horses play,/ Champ and chafe and toss in the spray. MATTHEW ARNOLD/ *THE FORSAKEN MERMAN*

Old-time temperance lecturers used to take a drunk along on their tours as a horrible example of what Demon Rum can do to a man. The ravaged creature would slouch in a chair on the stage while the lecturer championed sobriety by telling his audience what a promising citizen the exhibit had been before drink ruined him.

As a champion of unsullied beaches I have my own horrible examples, and they are chiefly in New Jersey. The beaches there are numerous, long and straight; they face the ocean squarely and they are made of the softest sand. About a century ago, when they teemed with shore and sea birds and had few visitors except commercial bird hunters, these beaches must have been incredibly graceful and serene. But the Jersey shore had the misfortune of being close to two large cities —New York and Philadelphia—and many smaller ones. Some beaches were right on the mainland; others were on peninsulas or barrier islands that were easy to get to even in the era before automobiles. Neither the state nor local governments seem to have made any effort to prevent the shortsighted exploitation that turned the shore into an eyesore. Many beaches in Delaware and Maryland suffered a similar fate and now run New Jersey's a close and sorry second. The millions of people who crowd these places rarely get a glimpse of a proper beach; about the only sights they see, if the traffic allows them to reach the beach at all, are boardwalks, sea walls, jetties and miles of huddled cottages with more ranks of cottages pressing as close behind them as lemmings crowding their way toward the sea.

But despite the prevalence of these settlements, some marvelously wild and near-wild beaches still fringe the Middle Atlantic shore from New York City to Virginia. One such beach runs an unbroken 37 miles along Assateague Island, paralleling the Maryland and Virginia coasts. Others are on the largely unfrequented barrier islands south of Assateague. In such havens the ocean rules the scene in its grand, immemorial way and the land responds with the subtle elegance of sand and dunes and beach grass.

Whether exploited or unspoiled, the beaches from New York Harbor southward share one critical attribute: they are not solid, dependable land, but shifting, dynamic boundaries between land and water. Scientists who study them do not entirely agree on how they were formed. They are not of direct glacial origin like the beaches of Cape Cod and Long Island. The glaciers stopped at New York in their move from the north, and provided no ready moraines to supply more southerly beaches with loose material. A longshore current, pushed by wind and waves and generally flowing toward the south, was, however, a factor in their formation. A glance at a map shows that many beaches in New Jersey, Delaware, Maryland and Virginia are peninsulas built by sand that the current laid down across bays and other coastal indentations.

A little of that sand may have come from northern moraines, leaking southward from New York, but most of it is probably of more local origin. The most widely accepted theory holds that the peninsula beaches are composed mainly of sandy material eroded from the edge of the land and washed into the sea. They have shifted their position many times in response to changes in sea level. When the ocean rose, as it did when the earth's icecaps diminished and released their water, it flooded the existing coast and carried sand inland to form new beaches with bays and marshes behind them. When the sea retreated, as it did during the ice ages, the beaches advanced. Sometimes these beaches and their dunes were established where there had been none before, while old dunes remained as ridges well away from the sea. This seems to have happened especially often on the Eastern Shore of Virginia, where many such ridges attest to the instability of the beaches.

At present the sea along the Middle Atlantic coast appears to be rising very slowly, at the rate of about 15 hundredths of an inch per year. If this rise continues, it will tend to make the beaches that are now on peninsulas or islands creep shoreward. Some of the salt marshes behind them will fill with sand and disappear; new marshes will form, filling bays and lagoons that are now open water. Other marshes and low-lying land may be covered with shallow water.

This prospect bodes ill in the long run for those sections of the coast that are heavily built up, but a greater and more immediate threat than the rising sea is the effect of constructions such as groins, jetties and breakwaters, which collect sand on one side while causing beaches on the other side to erode away. A trip down the coast from New York to Virginia shows many cases of potential or actual disaster. The waves slosh under boardwalks. Houses originally built on dune ridges now find themselves on the beach itself. Sea walls constructed at enormous cost to protect valuable real estate are being undermined, with no sand remaining to shield them from the buffeting of the surf.

Perhaps the most striking example of such beach erosion is at Ocean City, Maryland, where a long stone jetty has been built out to sea to keep a navigable channel open. For a short distance to the north of the jetty the beach has widened by some 800 feet. But still farther north the narrow sandy peninsula on which Ocean City stands is rapidly washing away. The foundations of many houses are below high-water mark, protected by flimsy wooden barriers. Some houses stand on piles with the waves breaking beneath them. The next big hurricane that comes along may not be kind to Ocean City. Because of the jetty, its beach is no longer free to move in response to natural forces without doing damage to man's structures.

Happily, there are a few beaches between New York and Virginia that still have freedom of movement. One of them is just south of Ocean City, straddling the Maryland-Virginia state line: the beach of Assateague Island, nearly houseless and roadless, much of its 37-mile length as wild as it was before Columbus first saw America. The greater part of Assateague has been a national seashore since 1965, and most likely its beauty will be preserved indefinitely. Here the waves beat their eternal rhythms, washing up to a high-water mark that is unlittered except for a few bits of flotsam from far away. On long stretches of the beach the only trace of man is an occasional ship hulk half buried in the sand, the rotting remains of a vessel that came to grief long ago on sandbars offshore. But there is plenty of evidence of wildlife, particularly migratory birds. In springtime sandpipers, plovers, curlews and other long-legged shore birds dance across the soft, trackless sand; colonies of sea birds, among them terns, black skimmers and laughing gulls (named for the loud, clear *ha-ha-ha* notes of their call) nest among the clumps of beach grass in summer; winter residents—ducks, geese and swans—flock in the ponds and marshes on the island's landward side.

In all, more than 275 kinds of birds have been identified on Assateague, both permanent local species and seasonal sojourners. One especially notable autumn visitor is the peregrine falcon, less formally known as the duck hawk. This is the same "noble peregrine" that was highly prized by Old World falconers long before America was discovered; and for a time it was captured on Assateague for taming and training by men who practiced that traditional sport of kings. The adult peregrine is a splendid-looking bird with a crown of black that fades to slate blue on its back; both the back and the cream-colored underside are barred with black. A short but sharply hooked beak, cruel talons and piercing eyes mark it as a hunter of other birds and occasionally small mammals. As a swift and daring flier it has few equals, and can sometimes be seen streaking out of the sky to snatch one of the ducks that congregate in the marshes behind Assateague.

Besides its flourishing bird population, Assateague is home to raccoons, red foxes, otters, muskrats, cottontail rabbits and deer. Some of the deer are small native whitetails standing only about three and a half feet high at the shoulder, but most of them are sika deer, a Japanese species. They are descendants of deer said to have been given to a Boy Scout troop by a large estate owner on the mainland. The Boy Scouts released them on the island in 1923. A sika is somewhat smaller than a whitetail, its face is not as long and its tawny coat, spotted with white along the spine, is denser. The sika has prospered wonderfully in Assateague's wilderness, browsing in forests of lofty, wide-spreading loblolly pines that grow on some of the higher land; the herds have increased to the point where the national seashore authorities have had to take steps to control their numbers.

Assateague Island looks like primeval wilderness, but it is actually something much more heartening. It is reclaimed wilderness. At one time there were four small settlements on the island, but by the turn of the century they had been largely abandoned. Many years later, in the 1950s, some 5,000 property lots were sold, about 50 houses were erected, and a paved road 10 miles long was built behind the beach of the Maryland section, extending to the Virginia line. The road was made of shells mixed with a small amount of asphalt and spread on soft sand, but it bore the impressive name of Baltimore Avenue.

Forming a graceful arc against the Atlantic surf, the northern end of Hog Island, off the Virginia coast, is a classic example of a barrier

beach constructed by the ocean's longshore current. As the current continues to deposit sand, this part of the island will lengthen further.

Then, in 1962, a mighty storm raged off Assateague. At the peak of high tide, huge waves rampaged across the island, which is mostly low lying, smashing houses to flinders and flushing the wreckage into Chincoteague Bay, between Assateague and the mainland. The storm amply demonstrated that the island was no place for a built-up resort. Today Baltimore Avenue is no more than an occasional crust of crumbling shell-flecked blacktop. Here and there can be seen a few chunks of concrete, part of the foundations of a house obliterated by the waves. I feel sympathy for the people who lost property but I also feel gratitude for the storm that battered Assateague back to its natural state.

Assateague National Seashore can now be reached by two routes. The more northerly is from Berlin, Maryland, over a road that crosses a marshy lagoon on a bridge and a causeway and ends on the Assateague shore a few miles beyond a small Maryland state park. The other approach is by bridge from the picturesque old village of Chincoteague (pronounced *shin-co-teague*) on Chincoteague Island, Virginia, which lies just inland from the southern end of Assateague.

Except for the state park, the Maryland part of Assateague is largely national seashore. The 12-mile stretch south of the park is open to people on foot and to approved beach vehicles, but a seashore area at the northern tip of the island is off limits to vehicles.

I traveled down the beach from the park to the Virginia line—marked only by a row of posts—with a park ranger. He was, as is usually the case, a friendly man full of love of nature and local information. The handful of people we saw on the beach were mostly surf fishermen sitting passively behind their rods watching the waves and waiting for a channel bass or a bluefish to bite.

Much of the time we went along the beach itself, which was slightly undulating; sometimes we switched to a faint track behind the beach, which revealed a few traces of Baltimore Avenue. Beyond the last fisherman the wide, untrodden beach led on and on, utterly deserted except for two or three raucous gulls gliding overhead. Back from the beach most of the land was low and covered with patches of gray-barked bayberry bushes between stretches of grass and bare sand. On Assateague, as wherever it grows, the bayberry's greenish-gray, aromatic, waxy fruit is a favorite food of numerous kinds of birds, and its evergreen foliage provides browsing for deer. The benefits of bayberry do not stop at this, of course. Early settlers along the Eastern seaboard ground the bark of its root into a powder that was believed to be effective in treat-

In search of food, a fast-flying black skimmer plows the waters of Virginia's Chincoteague Inlet. When its protruding, knifelike lower mandible strikes a fish such as a silversides, the skimmer's preferred diet, the short upper mandible clamps down to trap the prey. Still in full flight, the skimmer will pull its bill out of the water, straighten up and swallow the morsel. Often it will return to explore its own wake, scooping up other fish attracted by the movement of water.

ing colds, cuts and inflammations, and the berries are still used in making soap and candles.

A few miles north of the Virginia line we came to a slightly higher stretch of land with loblolly pines growing on it. "People lived here in the old days," said the ranger. We turned inland, being careful to stay on bare patches of soil so as not to damage the precious grass. The ground level rose perhaps 10 feet, but this was enough to change the character of the vegetation. We passed among high bushes, mostly myrtle and sumac, then came to an open forest where low spreading oaks mingled with the pines; some of them had grapevines twining among their branches. The forest glades were bright with iris and other wild flowers and russet-brown mats of fallen pine needles.

"A village called Green Run was around here somewhere," the ranger explained. "Fishermen mostly, but there were enough people to have a schoolhouse and even a small hotel. There's a graveyard too, with one gravestone left. The rest of the markers were cedarwood—vandals ruined them before the national seashore took over." Green Run's farmers had once tilled a total of nearly 60 acres, though now anything like arable soil is hard to find on Assateague. They also ran cattle, sheep and horses whose destructive grazing certainly contributed to the general bareness of the modern island.

At some time in the past the Maryland part of Assateague, now wooded only in spots, had considerable forests on it. Early reports tell of lumbering operations, and in the mid-18th Century a pirate, Charles Wilson, wrote to his brother revealing that he had buried chests of treasure on Assateague, on a "bluff facing the Atlantic Ocean with cedar trees growing on it about 1⅓ yards apart." Wilson's treasure has not been found, and if the bluff existed, it has long since blown or washed away.

There is a good chance that Assateague can be restored to its forested state merely by letting nature take its healing course. The young pines and oaks I saw looked healthy, and down the length of the island young bushes are pioneering in grassy places or even on bare sand.

Back at the northern end of Assateague, beyond the Maryland state park, the ranger and I came to a fence that extended clear across the island, a quarter of a mile wide at this point. We stopped at a gap in the fence with a chain across it and the ranger opened the padlock that held the chain so we could drive through. "This is actually private property," he said. "We patrol it some in our vehicles, but no one else is permitted to come here except by special permission from the National

Park Service." We snaked along a vague track among low sand hills and myrtle and sumac bushes, and after a few miles we reached the northern section of the seashore and cut across the dune line to the beach. The tide was low and we deliberately drove along close to the water. "The waves will wash our tracks out," said the ranger. "We like to keep it that way."

The area we were in was very low, with only the faintest scattering of beach grass growing on the sand all the way across the island to the salt marsh between Assateague and the mainland. "This was an inlet once," the ranger explained. "The sea washes over the beach sometimes, but we hope to build it up by putting snow fences across it to start sand collecting." Farther on, a dune line rose a few feet, and here bright green waving beach grass had taken full possession and was spreading its underground roots all around. "This is a nesting ground," the ranger told me. "We can take a look if we're careful."

As we walked toward the grassy area the sky was full of birds, mostly terns and black skimmers. One of the terns gave a sharp cry and made a power dive directly at my head. I knew from experience that it would not stab me with its sharp, threatening bill, but just the same I could not help dodging. "They dive-bomb you sometimes," said the ranger. A little later a black skimmer dipped down toward us and landed a gob of dung at our feet. "Near miss," the ranger grinned. "That's why the grass is so green around here."

Standing in the freshly fertilized grass, I felt nothing but admiration for the skimmer. Graceful and slender-winged, it is black only on top; the sides of its head, its underparts and its forked tail are snowy white. Its long sharp bill is red tipped with black, and in feeding it uses this bill in a unique way that explains why it is sometimes called a cutwater. The skimmer's diet is mainly small fish, which it usually catches on the wing, skimming close to the water with its bill open; the lower half of the bill—which is considerably longer than the upper half—cleaves the surface like a plow and scoops up the catch. When not occupied by the serious business of feeding, the skimmer will sometimes fly along with the lower part of its bill dangling open foolishly, as though the effort to close it were too great.

Among the clumps of grass on the dunes, resting in shallow depressions, were tern and black skimmer eggs, both dimly speckled to match the sand. "The folks from the mainland used to call this the 'egging grounds,' " the ranger said. "They would come over in boats and take away baskets of eggs to eat and sell. We've stopped that, and we've got a lot more birds now. There's one of the young skimmers." A sparrow-sized nestling with brown streaks that made it resemble a bunch of dead grass was crouched in a hollow; its parents had shaped this comfortable spot in the sand by squatting and turning around and around. "It won't move. Until they are big enough to run, nature tells the babies to hold still." I knelt and took a picture of the nestling from two feet away. It did not move so much as a quarter inch. As I stood up, I startled an older nestling, which dodged through the grass with amazing speed. "When nature gives them the word," said the ranger, "they can run like rats. They don't try to fly until they're old enough to be good at it. Let's get out of here. The birds are getting roused up." As we walked off, some of the skimmers followed us, swooping low on their narrow wings and making reproachful remarks.

North of the nesting ground the beach changed its character. It became narrower and steeper, backed by a sandy bank a few feet high with bare grass roots drooping out of it. "Erosion," said the ranger. "This end of Assateague is in trouble. It's that jetty at Ocean City Inlet. It stops the sand that ought to come to us." A little farther on, we could see across the inlet to Ocean City itself, its buildings tightly clustered at the end of its sandy peninsula.

The next day, with special permission, I walked to the beach beyond the private property alone. Now the beach was all my own, utterly virgin, not a print on it except the delicate embroidery made by the feet of little shore birds. Nothing looked different from the day before, but in my solitude the beach felt different. The air smelled pure; the shore on which the waves were breaking seemed as deserted as in the far-off time before even the first Indians settled along the Atlantic coast. I looked around for signs of man: there were none. No planes marred the sky, no boats the ocean. The emptiness of the beach made me feel all the more intimately tied to it. Everything I observed seemed focused with an extra intensity, as if I were looking through a microscope and a telescope at the same time.

All sorts of new details appeared to my sharpened eyes. I watched pinholes blowing bubbles when the swash of a wave flowed over dry sand; I had seen such bubbles many times before, but had never paid them special attention. At one place I discovered the waves cutting an indentation into the shoreline; a small roundish sandbar not far from shore was making the waves curve around it and was aiming their full force at the beach.

As the hours passed, I saw a magnificent thundercloud, perhaps four to five miles high, rising into the clear blue sky some distance away. First it was cauliflower-shaped; while I watched, it spread sideways and its top became flat, like that of an anvil, as it reached the bottom of the stratosphere—the usual upper limit of thunderclouds. But a few minutes later its flat top bulged upward, indicating that powerful vertical winds were pushing the cloud up past the limit. Such clouds are enormously violent, and soon I saw the flicker of lightning and heard the mutter of distant thunder.

I congratulated myself that I was not under that cloud, but within a few minutes my pleasure had given way to worry. Thunderclouds help to encourage the formation of other clouds ("cells," the meteorologists call them) nearby, and suddenly the clear sky above my head turned gray, then darker gray. I knew I was close to the base of a newly formed thundercloud; the top of my head was the highest thing around, and the human body is an excellent conductor of electricity. But at that point on the beach the dune line was about five feet high and offered a little protection, so I sat down near it to enjoy the storm.

And a marvelous spectacle it was, made all the more dramatic by the level, lonely beach. For a while there was no wind at all. The small ripples that normally rumple the backs of waves almost disappeared, and the waves remained glassy smooth until their moment of breaking. They seemed subtly hushed as they broke; perhaps the silence was a product of my imagination, perhaps the result of the absence of wind sounds. Then patches of the sea turned an ominous dark gray blue as savage squalls raced across them. When the squalls hit the beach they raised stinging sheets of sand. Air sucked into the base of the rising cloud had caused these squalls, and I knew they would soon be followed by gusts flowing in the other direction as air in the core of the cloud was dragged down by raindrops. I had observed such spreading gusts often before, but usually where hills and other surface irregularities impeded them. This time there was nothing to interfere with their driving movement. The spectacle unfolded in its classic stages. Lightning flashed and flowed like rivers of light. Nearby thunder cracked and boomed. The gusts blew with mighty force; rain frosted the sea and made the sand boil at my feet.

I walked back to the Maryland state park wet as a fish but deeply satisfied. Never before had I enjoyed a thunderstorm so much. It was like hearing a burly basso standing on an empty stage in an empty auditorium and filling it with his voice. I commend the experience to anyone who does not mind risking the danger of being struck by lightning. All that is needed is a lonely beach, a shipless sea and a vigorous thundercloud overhead.

The southern part of Assateague Island is federal property, but it has a complex relationship to the government, and its nomenclature is confusing. The extreme southern tip of the island is administered by the National Park Service although it is part of the Chincoteague National Wildlife Refuge (none of which is on Chincoteague Island), which is run by the Fish and Wildlife Service.

The most interesting fact about southern Assateague is its youth; geologically speaking, it is almost newborn. An attractive theory suggests that only a few thousand years ago Chincoteague Island, now on the inland side of Assateague, faced the open ocean. Parallel ridges, presumably traces of ancient shifting shorelines, indicate that it may have done so for many thousand years, while the ocean level rose and fell. Then the current pushing down the coast from the northeast formed a sandspit seaward of Chincoteague. Gradually the sandspit grew and swelled into a barrier island with salt marshes rising behind it. By 1850 this former sandspit—Assateague—had come between Chincoteague and the sea. The ambitious young island kept growing, and in time formed, on its southernmost end, what is now called Fishermen's Point—a four-mile-long hook of land that curves around Assateague Cove, more commonly known as Tom's Cove. This place was once the principal source of the large and succulent Chincoteague oysters prized by gourmets for their delicate flavor. Today most so-called Chincoteague oysters come from Chesapeake Bay, although some are still cultivated in beds off Assateague.

With a ranger I went out on Fishermen's Point, past a Coast Guard station that was built near the tip in 1922 but is now—because of the continued growth of the beach—two and a half miles away from it. The beach here is so new that salt marsh has not had time to develop behind it, though soft sediment is accumulating and soon marsh grasses will take hold. Beach grass is already thriving near the tip, and sea birds have found a safe new nesting ground in a place that was covered by salt water no more than five years ago.

No account of Assateague would be complete without some mention of its most highly publicized wildlife—the wild ponies that were made nationally famous by Marguerite Henry's popular novel *Misty of Chincoteague,* which also was made into a movie in 1961. Various legends account for the ponies' origin. The novel has them escaping from a Spanish ship in the 1500s; another theory claims that pirates brought the animals ashore. The likeliest explanation is that they are descendants of livestock that grazed on and often ruined many barrier islands up and down the Atlantic coast; this theory gets added credence from the fact that a few wild ponies are also to be found on Ocracoke Island off the coast of North Carolina. In the past—as far back as Revolutionary times and perhaps even earlier—most of Assateague was a common grazing ground like the open range of the Old West, where horses belonging to many owners roamed at will and were rounded up once a year for branding and marketing.

The roundup, called "penning," is still an annual event, and some claim it is the oldest ritual of its kind in the United States. It used to be an uproarious occasion. One eyewitness in the early 1800s reported the literal depopulation of the neighboring islands as their inhabitants flocked to Assateague to see "the mad flight of wild horses careering away along a narrow, naked, level, sand-beach at the top of their speed, with manes and tails waving in the wind before a company of mounted men, upon the fleetest steeds, shouting and hallowing in the wildest notes of triumph, and forcing the affrighted animals into the angular pen of pine logs . . . and then the deafening peals of loud hurras from the thousand half-frenzied spectators, crowding into a solid mass around the enclosure, to behold the beautiful wild horse, in all his native vigor subdued by man. . . ."

There are not many wild ponies on Assateague now. A few live at the Maryland end; while I was there one of them wandered into the state park and bit a girl. Most of them are in the wildlife refuge on the Virginia part of the island, where they can often be seen grazing on the salt marshes. They look healthy and well suited to their wilderness life, despite limited fresh water, such nonnutritious fodder as marsh grass, harsh winter weather and summertime swarms of pestering flies that drive them into the surf for relief. In size the animals range between a standard horse and a Shetland pony. Formerly they were even smaller, stunted by the rigors of their environment, but about 50 years ago they began to grow slightly larger as their mares were deliberately bred to standard-sized stallions. Such crossbreeding also brought changes in color to the long shaggy coats. These used to be black, bay or sometimes sorrel or gray; half of the ponies today are piebald or mottled like pintos.

The Assateague ponies do not congregate in a single herd but live in

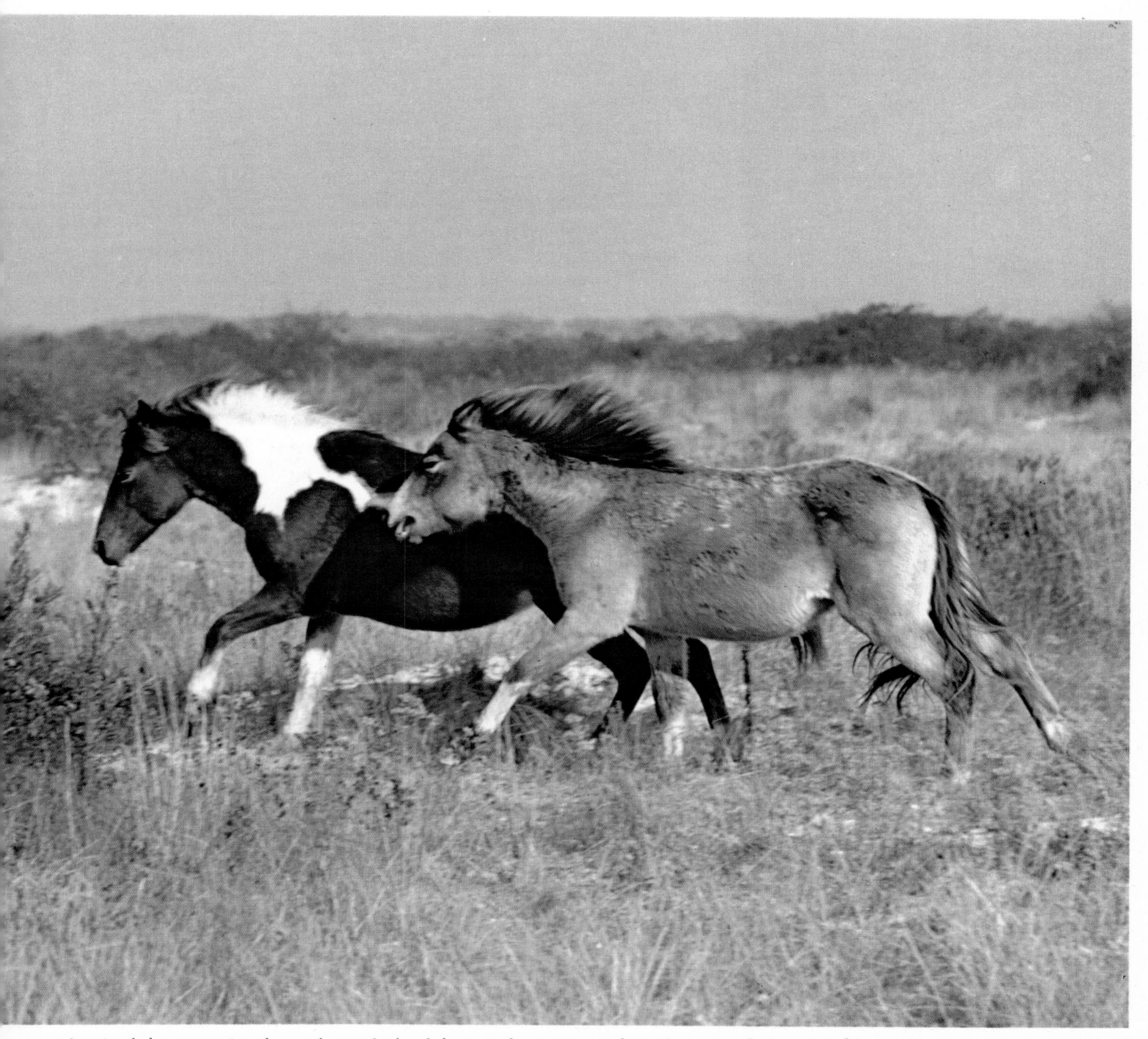

A pair of shaggy ponies, descendants of a herd that may have swum ashore from a 16th Century shipwreck, roams Assateague Island.

isolated groups ranging from eight or 10 up to about 20. Each group roams a fairly well-defined territory of its own choosing and is dominated by one or more stallions with harems of mares that they guard with ferocious jealousy. The Fish and Wildlife Service now limits the ponies in the wildlife refuge to about 150 in order to preserve a balance between them and their habitat. All these animals belong to the Chincoteague Volunteer Fire Department, which organizes the modern version of the annual penning.

A few miles south of Assateague begins an extraordinary chain of barrier islands 50 miles long. They start close to the narrow peninsula that forms the Eastern Shore of Virginia and gradually move away from it until they stand five miles out to sea. Though some are backed by salt marshes and others boast small forests, the barrier islands are remarkably unstable; they wash away and build up, form and re-form almost as if they were sandbars in a flooding river. And they are amazingly wild. Although almost 40 per cent of the population of the United States lives within a day's drive of the islands, they have no permanent inhabitants except a few Coast Guardsmen. Seldom do their broad beaches show a human footprint; the great clouds of birds that nest on them—including such rare species as the snowy egret and the glossy ibis—are left undisturbed.

I had never been on these mysterious islands, so I persuaded an agreeable and knowledgeable employee of the Virginia Institute of Marine Science at Wachapreague, on the mainland, to transport me there in a flat-bottomed aluminum outboard motorboat. Our first destination was Hog Island, most of which was recently bought by the Nature Conservancy, a privately supported organization whose purpose is to protect unspoiled natural areas from exploitation; the group owns four other islands in this chain. Our boat crossed a wide, shallow bay and wound through narrow channels in a salt marsh where flocks of skimmers, gulls and terns were roosting. The landscape ahead was empty and almost as flat as the ocean. From our vantage point, some of the islands were identifiable only by thin lines of beach greenery; others loomed comparatively high, with tall timber growing on them. At one place, off the southern end of Hog Island, was a line of dazzling white where the sea was breaking on a shoal.

We landed on the marsh side of Hog Island, startling several long-legged American oyster catchers; ordinarily these large black-and-white wading birds feed on the open beach, where they probe the sand with long, bright red bills for their favorite shellfish. A walk of nearly a mile through grass, scattered myrtle bushes and some loblolly pines brought us to a dramatic beach on the island's seaward side. Hog Island is about six miles long. The north end is rapidly building out to sea, and the recently formed beach there is bare, flat and about a quarter of a mile wide. Beyond it is an even newer curving bar enclosing a lagoon two feet deep. I waded across it and arrived at the outer bar at the moment when the rising tide broke through it. I watched as the waves quickly cut a channel and sea water raced into the lagoon, widening and deepening the channel and making great swirls in the still water of the lagoon. It was a striking demonstration in miniature of the natural forces that cut inlets through barrier beaches.

From Hog Island we went to nearby Parramore, the largest of the offshore islands, much of which is covered with tall pine forest. Not a Nature Conservancy property, Parramore is privately owned but happily almost nothing has been done to tame it. A weed-grown road leads from a landing on the marsh side through the woods to a former lifesaving station that has been turned into a lodge for duck hunters. Unoccupied most of the year, this place looked rather neglected when I saw it. The beach beyond is eroding, but this is something comparatively new. Not many years ago it was advancing rapidly out to sea. The lifesaving station, which was built in the days when launching boats through the surf was the technique used to help a ship in distress, was abandoned because the beach moved too far away from it.

As I learned the following day, the best way to see how these islands have established themselves is not from a boat but from a slow, low-flying airplane. Smith Island, the southernmost in the chain (except for Fisherman's Island, which is crossed by the bridge-tunnel across the mouth of Chesapeake Bay) actually consists of two islands. One of them has at least 10 parallel stands of timber, mostly loblolly pines with shallow sloughs or marshes between them. Presumably each of these wooded ridges was once a sandbank behind a beach. Grass growing on the bank collected more sand and built it up to a height that could support timber. Then the beach widened, as I had seen it doing on Hog Island. A new grassy beach bank formed, grew higher, acquired timber and repeated the process. Such wooded ridges are also visible on other islands in the chain.

The mobility of Virginia's barrier islands seems to assure their continuance as unspoiled wilderness. So far attempts to build permanently on them have had unhappy endings. The most notable example concerns Hog Island. Until the 1930s a village of 300 to 500 people flourished at its southern end. It had two-story houses, streets, a school, a church, a post office, two stores and a graveyard. I talked with a group of its former inhabitants at a fish pier in a harbor on the mainland. A special breed of men, salty and amiable, they are quite willing to talk about their lost paradise, usually with a twinkle in the eye that shows they do not expect to be wholly believed. One of them was an old man with a handsome, weatherbeaten face. The others were younger but not young. I asked who had founded their village.

"Bad people," the old man said. "They were Australians. They were so bad they were thrown out of Australia."

I asked how old the village had been.

"Old enough to have ghosts," another one of the Hog Islanders told me, "and it takes a good while for ghosts to come around. One of them lived in a hollow tree."

"One of those ghosts lived in my father's house," the old man said. "It pestered us all the time."

I asked what the village looked like.

"It was real pretty," the old man told me. "We all had trees and gardens. The island had woods on it then, higher than on Parramore now. The town was two miles behind the beach. We had to walk through the woods to get there."

"We never had a murder on Hog Island," said another man, "and no one ever got drowned." He smiled. "All the men were gentlemen, and all the women were ladies."

The others laughed. "That's not what I remember. The girls were the prettiest and wildest on the Eastern Shore of Virginia. Young fellers came to the island just to court with 'em."

"We had some powerful men," said the old man. "One came when he was just a boy, sailing a schooner with his father. It seems they had a misunderstanding, so the boy figured it was best to climb up the mast. His old man went below to get his gun and shoot him out of the rigging. So the boy dove overboard and hung to the rudder all night. Next morning he swum five miles to Hog Island. He grew to be the most powerful man we ever had. He could take a line in his teeth and swim along dragging a schooner against a two-knot current."

All the Hog Islanders were smiling now. "I remember," said one, "when a schooner broke up on a bar. The tide was down and we could see her anchor sticking in the sand. So we told this feller—he was grown then—to go get it. We said it weighed only five hundred pounds, so he could handle it easy. He waded out in the waves, picked up that anchor and carried it ashore. Then we all had to laugh. We told him it weighed eleven hundred, not five hundred pounds. He was so sore he dropped it right down in the street, and no one else could budge it."

"What happened to the town?" I asked.

The smiles left their faces. "Well," said one, "something changed. We don't know what it was, but the beach started coming closer. The sea washed the land away, and the wind blew the trees down. Every year the breakers came closer and closer. Then came the hurricane of 1933, the first real bad one we'd had in a long time. The water came over the whole island, not waves, just water flowing among the houses. It washed one house into the bay and damaged others. We began to figure we'd better move."

"Neighbors helped each other," another man joined in. "Some houses were took apart, carried across the bay and set up again. Or sometimes they'd lash two barges together and float a whole house across. They put them up all along the shore. There's one of them now." He pointed across the street to a two-story house freshly painted green. "There's more of them down the road. They make us Hog Islanders kind of feel at home."

"My father didn't move our house," said the old man. "He left it to wash away with the ghost in it."

"Ghosts don't mind," said another man. They were all smiling again. "They find places to go. The ghost that lived in the hollow tree is still out there somewhere."

While building up the northern end of Hog Island, the sea had washed away the entire southern end. The site of the village is now hard to distinguish, and the stumps of its trees and its graveyard are under water.

Hog Island is still beautiful, perhaps more beautiful in its reversion to nature than it was when the wild girls and powerful men lived there. The island's beaches are pristine; the marshes behind them are a teeming nursery for fish and shellfish, and sea birds nest by thousands in its green, green grass. Its history should give pause to anyone who is minded to build on Virginia's lovely but fickle offshore islands.

5/ Domain of the Tides

Ye marshes, how candid and simple and nothing-withholding and free/ Ye publish yourselves to the sky and offer yourselves to the sea! SIDNEY LANIER/ *THE MARSHES OF GLYNN*

Dank, monotonous and malodorous—a place of muck and mosquitoes and ravenous greenhead flies, arrow-pointed stubble and sharp-bladed grass to cut the feet and slash the legs. So a salt marsh seems to many people, and they are happy to pass it by. Yet to me, the marshes between Cape Cod and Cape Lookout convey a very special kind of beauty, duplicated nowhere else. Picture a wonderfully smooth green lawn that may extend for miles and miles, ribboned with channels of blue water where the tide flows in and out; in autumn the green of the lawn turns russet yellow, but the serene harmony of color remains.

Not all of the beauty of a marsh, however, meets the eye: a good part of it is sensed rather than seen. In the middle of a big salt marsh one has a strange and satisfying feeling of isolation. You can look a long way in all directions without seeing a trace of man or his works. The air is full of the rich smell of salt water and vegetation—marsh grasses, sedges, rushes, cattails, algae. Except for the whisper of the wind, the murmur of the tide or the occasional call of a bird, the marsh is usually devoid of sound. This does not mean that marshes are empty of life. On the contrary, they swarm with living things—from animals as large as raccoons to creatures visible only under a microscope—that spend part or all of their lives hidden in or under the mat of the marsh grass or in the mud of the marsh bottom.

Though the grasses dominate the level green table of the marsh, its edges support a tremendous variety of other plants. These range from mainland and beach-growing types like bayberry and beach plum, sea lavender and seaside goldenrod to species that prefer damper and saltier environments—rushes, marshmallow with its hollyhocklike blossoms, thickets of marsh elder that can grow up to 12 feet tall, and the hardy, fleshy marsh samphire.

When viewed from the upland, most salt marshes look as even as well-clipped lawns. But when you investigate them closely, you find many irregularities. Among these are "pond holes," round or roundish pools roughly 10 to 20 feet across and a foot or so deep, where no grass grows. One theory holds that they were once stretches of open water that were surrounded, perhaps a thousand years ago, by the marsh, and that since then have diminished to their present status.

Everywhere in the marsh are the curving tidal creeks, whose bottoms are sometimes deep, soft mud, sometimes muddy sand where clams repose: soft-shelled ones with long necks, thick-shelled quahogs, razor clams with long narrow shells—all of them delicious to eat. The creeks also offer a lazy, tranquil kind of canoeing, which is one of the best ways to observe the life of a salt marsh. If you time things right, you can launch your canoe at the mouth of a creek on a rising tide and be carried with hardly a paddle stroke all the way to the distant upland, which may be several miles away. When the tide turns, it will carry you seaward again. A more complicated maneuver is to start at the upland end of the creek and let the ebbing tide carry you down to the confluence of another creek branch. Then when the tide turns, you can make it carry you up to the head of the second creek. I used to do this when I was a boy, sometimes spending most of a day drifting silently and in splendid solitude through the creeks, stopping from time to time to dig clams. Sometimes I fished for flounder that had come into the marsh to feed and whose platter-shaped outline I could dimly see as they lurked in the mud with only their eyes uncovered. If I worked it right I could ride on the tides through miles of marshland wilderness and be carried effortlessly back to my starting place.

Anyone who has ever been stranded, canoe aground in the mud, by a fast-ebbing tide, knows that its daily flow is the most visibly dynamic aspect of the marsh. It is literally the engine that drives the marsh's vital mechanisms, nourishing all its forms of life in one way or another. It is also the master builder of the marsh, carrying sand and silt into the open area behind a barrier beach where salt-adapted grasses can take hold. Once established, the grasses continue the work of marsh

building. Gradually, as generations of grasses flourish and die, the rotting stems and roots build up a smooth deposit of peat—partially decomposed vegetable matter mixed with silt washed from the upland. The peat accumulates to the level of normal high tides.

The grasses that provide the bulk of marsh peat are two closely related strains that, unlike most grasses, can live with their roots in sea water—*Spartina alterniflora* and *Spartina patens*. *Alterniflora* is a tall coarse grass that prefers to grow close to tidal bays and creeks where its roots are bathed in flowing sea water the greater part of the time. *Patens,* which is low growing, with narrow wiry stems and blades, prefers slightly higher marshland that is not covered by the tides for as long a period each day. It is most at home on Northern marshes and forms a springy turf that will support a man. In the South *patens* is less common. Virginia marshes, for instance, are mostly covered with *alterniflora*. Between its stems is bare, soft mud, not elastic turf; such marshes are difficult to walk on.

Spartina grasses have evolved so as to be able to live in their salty world, and the principal adaptive measure taken by these hardy plants is truly remarkable. Most plants that are immersed in salt water die —not as a direct consequence of exposure to salt, but because of the difference between the salt concentration of sea water and that of the water contained in most plant cells. Wetted by sea water, the relatively salt-free water inside the plant tends to flow toward the much more highly salted tidal water. It does this in obedience to simple laws of physics—a weak solution will always filter through a wet membrane toward a strong one—but the result is the dehydration, and death, of the plant. *Spartina* has beaten these laws by storing higher concentrations of salt in its cells than those that occur in sea water. With the salt balance rigged in its favor, it takes water from the sea and survives.

Alterniflora is sometimes called thatch, presumably because it was once used for thatching roofs. On Cape Cod, the common name for *patens* is salt hay. Until the early 20th Century it was extensively mowed for hay. In colonial days when someone asked a Cape Cod farmer for hay he got salt hay. If he wanted hay from upland fields he asked for English hay; common hay grasses were not native to heavily forested New England, and their seed was imported from the Old Country.

I can remember when hay was still mowed on Barnstable Great Marsh on Cape Cod. It was a chancy business; the cut grass might be floated away by an extra-high tide before it had time to dry. If this did not hap-

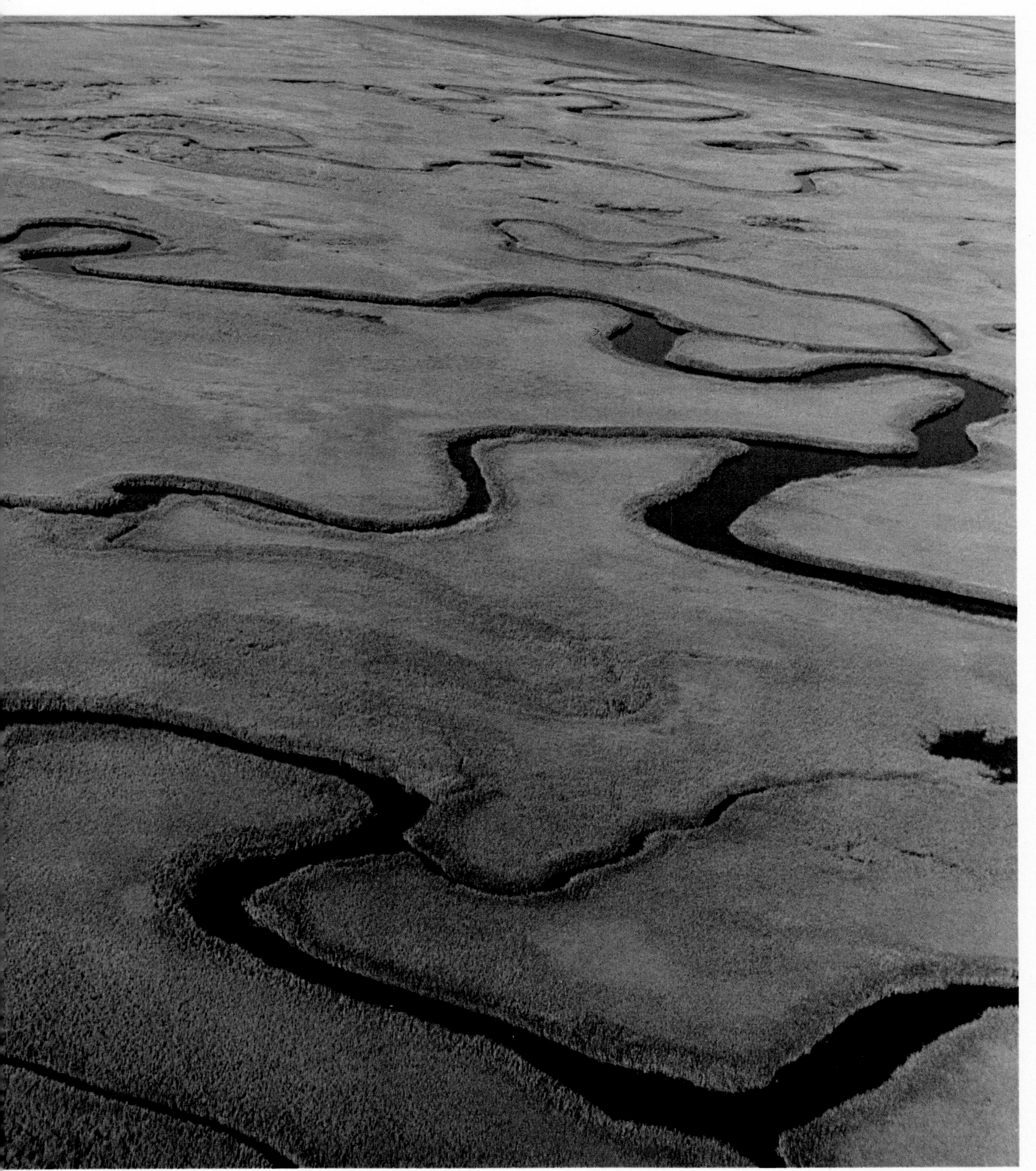

Tidal creeks meander through tall cordgrass in a Virginia salt marsh.

pen, the cured hay was piled in rounded stacks on circles of posts called staddles that held it above the storm tides; the stacks were kept from blowing off the staddles by long wooden rails leaned against the hay. These marsh stacks were wonderfully picturesque, sticking up out of the green expanse like the dwellings of some tribe of aborigines.

The *Spartina* grasses can change the geography of a shoreline with remarkable speed. A salt marsh may be thousands of years old, but new grassy patches and islands make their appearance on its fringes every year and can become established in as little as five years. The seeds of *alterniflora* are the pioneers. They colonize any place that is high enough to stay above the level of low tide for a few hours. The seeds grow into tall green stems and rootlike underground extensions spread sideways and send up other stems. Water flowing among them slows down and deposits sediment, and the surface that supports the grass rises higher.

When *alterniflora* has created a good-sized piece of marsh, the surface among the grass stems rises by sedimentation until a high tide will cover it only about half of the time. At this point *alterniflora*, which thrives when its roots are in contact with free-flowing sea water, ceases to grow with its accustomed vigor. It retreats to the tidal-creek margins and yields the higher marsh ground to *patens*, which forms a characteristically thick turf and builds up layers of nearly pure organic peat. In time the carpet of peat thickens until it reaches a level covered only by the extra-high tides that come with the full and new moons. At this point upward growth of the "high marsh" slows; the dense *patens* turf is as healthy as ever, but in the heat of summer most of the organic matter that it produces decays entirely or is flushed away by the high tides instead of turning to peat.

Except on the high marsh near its borders, you will probably see few mammals; they do not like the prospect of being caught far from dry land by a flood tide. Mink, which are at home in the water, are one of the exceptions, and the larger marshes support a good number of them. On high spots you can sometimes see the nests of grasses where mink bear and raise their young. Their lithe, long bodies clad in silky brown fur, the mink feed on mussels, clams, crabs and unwary birds. If you are lucky, you may be entertained by a pair of lighthearted otters, relatives of the mink, as they frolic in the creeks, sliding down the mudbanks and using their webbed hind feet to propel themselves through the water with astonishing agility. Raccoons also like the marshes and venture out on them at low tide for their share of mussels

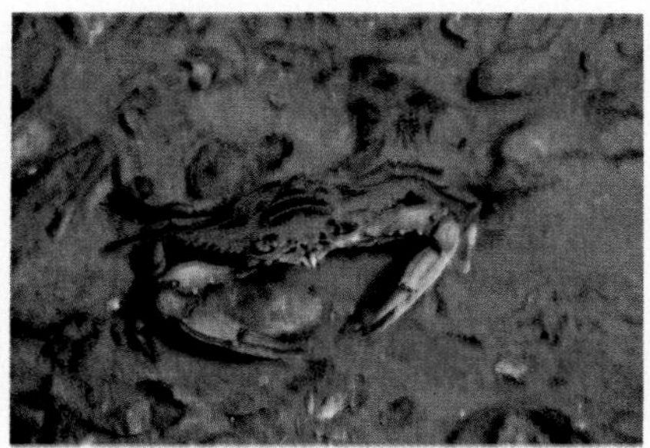

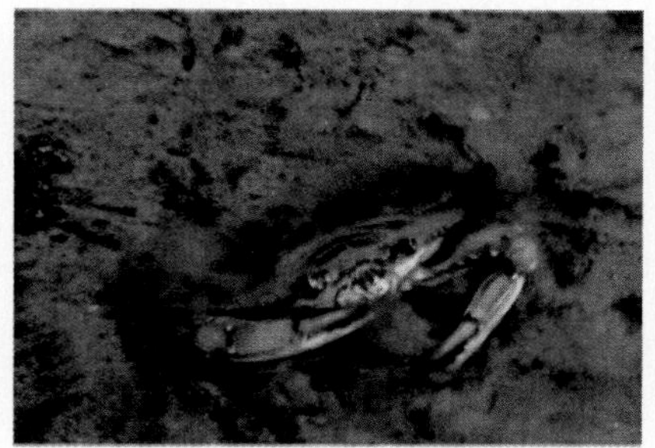

A North Carolina blue crab's strategy for ambushing its prey is illustrated in this sequence of pictures. At top, the crab prepares to dig into the mud of a tidal creek bottom. In the middle picture, it backs into the mud, using its front legs to loosen the soil while its paddlelike hind legs shovel out the silt, sand and clay. At bottom, the crab is shown with its whole body concealed —except for eyes and a small patch of shell. Thus entrenched, the crab will snap up any small fish or crustacean that ventures within reach of its claws.

and crabs. Sometimes they stay for several days in spite of the tides, bedding down on bunches of dry grass.

The tides are, of course, no problem for birds; they simply fly away when tide conditions do not suit them. But more often than not conditions do suit them. Salt marshes teem with birds—ranging in size from great blue herons, which stand almost four feet tall, to tiny long-billed marsh wrens, which weave cosy nests in the high grass. Ducks of all kinds feed in the marshes; slender rails run nimbly through the grass stems; terns dive for fish in the creeks, and in more southerly marshes elegant white egrets stalk insects, minnows and shrimp in the shallows. Except for the gulls that wheel overhead, none of these birds are conspicuous until you have penetrated—preferably in a canoe, and silently—some distance into a marsh. There the birds will be going about their business, confident that no human being is near. They will look at you with surprise and some resentment, and slowly fly away.

Most of the birds are visitors that do not breed on the marsh. The permanent, year-round population of snails, worms, crabs, spiders and insects lives, basically, on the marsh grass and the algae and other microscopic plants that grow among its stems. The larder bulges. Various estimates have been made of the amount of organic material that a salt marsh produces annually. Some of them run as high as 10 tons (figured as dry matter) per acre. Most estimates are lower, but all scientists agree that a natural salt marsh produces as much food for animal life as good, well-cultivated agricultural land.

The cycle of food production begins with the death of the marsh grasses. On the high marsh the stems and blades of the *patens* grow so close together that no bare soil can be seen among them. In autumn they subside and form a resilient, feltlike mat that slowly decays from the bottom up. The tall stems of *alterniflora* behave differently; they break off in fall, leaving short stubble, and the straw floats away on the tide to pile up in windrows on the borders of the marsh.

Under the mats of *patens* or the windrows of *alterniflora* you will find many kinds of small creatures whose diets depend upon the slowly decomposing grass. If your vision were microscopic you would see many more, for the first creatures to benefit from the dead stems and blades are bacteria that can digest the tough cellulose of which the grasses are largely made. Larger organisms including certain types of protozoa multiply by eating the bacteria. The grass stems become covered with a layer of slime containing edible microscopic matter that many creatures find nutritious and presumably tasty. Tiny snails creep on the stems scraping them clean with their rasplike tongues. Crabs grapple a stem in their claws and pass it in front of their mouths, then work the food over with the small modified legs that serve them as cutlery. Decayed grass sinks into the mud and is swallowed by worms.

While microorganisms and small animals are reducing the grass to edible form, algae grow wherever they can, adding to the food supply. On some marshes the algae probably produce a quarter as much edible matter as the grass does. If you want to see algae at work, look for one of the round pond holes where no grass grows. You will probably see its bottom covered with a continuous dark green sheet of matted algae. When the sun is shining, the mat will be dotted with small bright droplets that look like dabs of mercury. They are bubbles of oxygen produced by the algae as they create organic matter out of carbon dioxide and water with the help of the energy of sunlight. Sometimes the bubbles get so numerous that they float the whole algae mat up to the surface of the pond hole.

The interaction of decayed matter with living things produces a rich organic detritus, a mixture of plant fragments, algae, bacteria and other microorganisms, living and dead. Through the detritus burrow tiny worms and the larvae of flies. Fiddler crabs, the males armed with one disproportionately huge claw—the "fiddle"—come out of their holes to scoop up this detritus and manipulate it with their mouth parts to get rid of the large particles before they swallow the remainder. Certain fish, including mullet and menhaden, whose bait-sized young live in the relatively safe water of the salt marsh, swallow the detritus whole. What passes through the alimentary canal of one creature is food for others in an almost endless process.

Not all the detritus stays in the marsh where it originated. When the tide is high, much of it gets mixed in with the flowing sea water and is carried into the creeks where clams, mussels and oysters filter it from the water as it passes over their gills. Such little fish as the mummichog, camouflaged by its muddy green color, and the silverside also feast on it. Bigger fish feed on the little fish. All take some nourishment out of the detritus, but some of it is left to wash into the open ocean, where it nourishes all sorts of sea creatures, large and small, that never come near a salt marsh.

Much has been made by conservationists of the function of salt marshes as the "nurseries of the sea"—perhaps too much; the world's richest fishing grounds, such as the Grand Banks and the coast of Peru, are

A greenhead fly perches on salt-specked marsh grass. The female of the species is a fierce biter, needing blood protein for her eggs.

stocked with deep-water species that have nothing to do with marshes. Nevertheless, salt marshes do have an important role to play in the ecology of the adjacent shore. They produce food for shellfish that abound in the coastal waters near them, and the tidal estuaries that drain them support many kinds of sport and commercial fish that would not be there if it were not for the prey that they find. The highly prized striped bass, for instance, spends its vulnerable youth in marsh estuaries feeding on mullet and menhaden.

Blue crabs, fiddler crabs and mud crabs are caught near salt marshes. From Delaware southward through Georgia, blue crabs are especially plentiful and provide a relaxed kind of fishing that appeals to many. All that a crab fisherman needs is a small dip net, a length of string and a piece of bait, preferably a chicken neck. He selects a marsh site with a patch of open water next to it and tosses the chicken neck out on the water as far as it will go on the end of the string. Then he sits down (a box or folding chair is useful) and contemplates the wilderness glories of grasses and tidal channels. He may wait quite a while before he feels a gentle tugging on the string. This means that a crab has grabbed the chicken neck in its needle-sharp claws.

The crab is not hooked, but clings stubbornly to the chicken neck as it is gently pulled in. The crab may even hold tighter, as if the bait were a living prey trying to escape. When the crab gets close enough, the fisherman stands up, peers into the water, lifts his catch off the bottom and slips the dip net under it. There is not much meat in a single crab, but a lucky fisherman may catch a bucketful in the course of an afternoon, in which case he should silently thank the salt marsh, which produces an endless annual supply of them.

Most clams and oysters are indirect products of salt marshes. They breed most plentifully in shallow water that has picked up nutrients from a marsh. The diamondback terrapin, a delicacy once so abundant in Southern and Middle Atlantic marshes that people got sick of eating them, can still be found. Ducks and other waterfowl depend on marshes. Some of them nest there; others use marshes as sources of vegetable and animal food during their migrations. One reason wild ducks are not as plentiful as in former times is the widespread destruction of their nesting areas in marshes by dredging, filling and pollution along the whole populous shoreline.

Not long after it became general knowledge that mosquitoes breed in still water men began digging ditches to flush the marsh with tidal water and drain the pond holes. This didn't do much good. Indeed the mosquito, followed closely by the greenhead, is the most conspicuously and annoyingly numerous marsh insect. In lesser quantities there are some 400 species of other insects to be found in marshes. Most of the insects are grasshoppers, flies and even ants that venture to the marsh border from the upland to feed on the grass and dried detritus. Beetles and spiders prey on these plant-eating insects. Most such creatures live only part of their lives on the marsh; they escape the tide by crawling up grass stems or burrowing inside them, where there is always some air; some can even survive under water for a while by remaining motionless and shutting their air holes, and living in a kind of suspension until the tide turns.

Most are thus adaptable to normal conditions of life on the marsh. But few—and I find this curiously fitting—are as closely tied throughout their lives to the salty world of the marsh as the biting insects. Mosquito larvae, often in numbers sufficient to darken the surface of a pond hole, are aquatic creatures for part of their lives. Greenhead larvae root through the detritus before emerging to vie with the mosquitoes for honors as the most bloodthirsty of insects. Maddening as these pests are, however, they may have their benign side—as unwitting protectors of the marsh wilderness from crowds of people. Walking, canoeing and swimming in the marsh—at high tide the creek water is deeply, refreshingly cold—can be among the most satisfying of experiences. But the biters exact a price, and they seem to love the taste of human blood more than anything else.

Salt-Marsh Country

The Middle Atlantic coast abounds with wild and beautiful salt marshes. They snuggle securely, protected against the pounding of the open ocean, behind a string of sandy barrier islands that stretches southward from New Jersey through Delaware and Maryland, and down the Virginia capes. While Cape Cod and Long Island have a few impressive salt marshes, this more southerly coast possesses dozens of large green multichanneled wetlands. Virginia alone has 100,000 acres of salt marsh.

These southerly salt marshes were all formed the same way. First came the barrier islands, created when the last glacial ice sheet melted and the level of the world's oceans rose. The climate became wetter and erosion of the land increased. Laden with this eroded inland material, strong longshore currents eventually built high-duned beaches along this part of the Atlantic coast. Then the sea, continuing to rise, cut through the dunes and flooded the low-lying areas behind them. But the dunes remained, protecting the flooded backwaters from the breakers and winds of the sea. Slowly the sluggish backwaters deposited silt, the water became shallower—and salt marshes were born, including the one on the opposite page, behind Virginia's Hog Island.

When well protected, a salt marsh will build itself. The key materials are two kinds of grass, *Spartina alterniflora,* called cordgrass, and a relative, *Spartina patens.* They are among the very few plants that thrive in salt water although cordgrass—which is taller and tougher—can stand more frequent flooding. As a result, it predominates in the watery Middle Atlantic marshes while *patens* dominates the higher marshes farther north. The cordgrass drives its roots into silt that is above water at low tide. It both anchors the silt and creates dense layers of peat as its old roots die and new ones grow above them. In some old marshes the peat is 26 feet deep.

The look of a typical salt marsh—a gently waving green expanse through which channels of greenish-brown water twist and turn—is magnificently wild yet peaceful. But this serenity does not prevail down around the roots of the grass and in the mudbanks. Here swarm masses of crawling, swimming, burrowing creatures that eat tons of vegetable matter produced by the marsh grasses and that in turn form the base of the food chain of the shore.

White-topped Atlantic waves rumble toward the narrow south end of Hog Island, one of the sandy barriers off the Virginia coast. Though itself vulnerable to the power of the wind and sea, the island—stabilized in part by sand-anchoring beach grass—serves as an effective shield for the low-lying area behind it: a six-mile-wide expanse of salt marsh, mud flats and bays laced by the shallow channels of tidal streams.

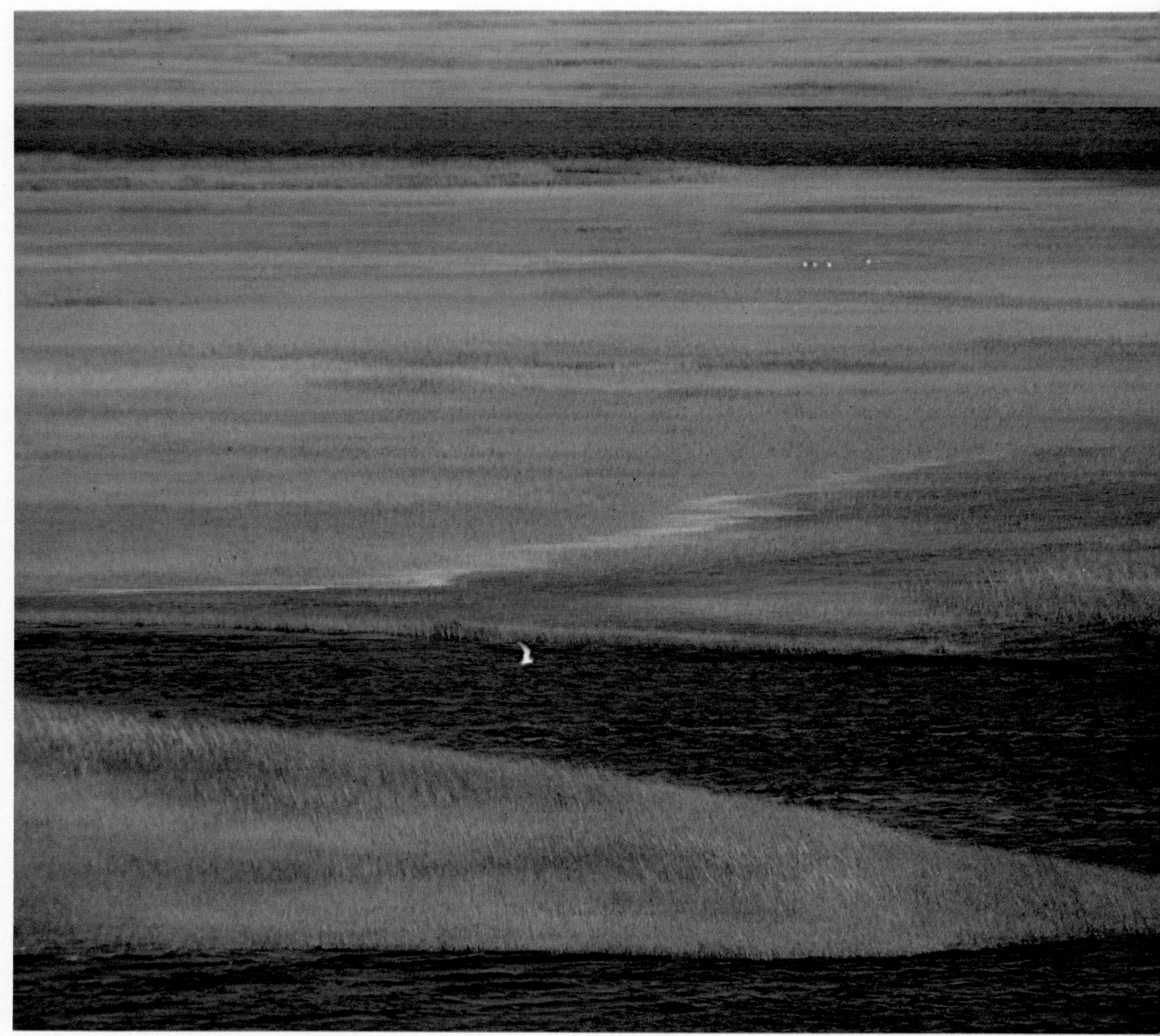

THE SALT MARSH OF CEDAR ISLAND–HIGH TIDE

Ebb and Flow on a Virginia Marsh

At high tide the salt marsh behind Cedar Island, nine miles north of Hog Island, is almost entirely awash *(left)*. Only the tips of the tall cordgrass are visible, bending with the water's flow as terns gather to fish in the flooded flats. Because of the deep twice-daily inundation, little but cordgrass grows here—and it is primarily cordgrass that keeps the marsh's mud and peat from eroding, as the picture at right shows.

The mudbank in the foreground, though undermined by the tide, holds up because it is knit together by the cordgrass' extensive root system. Another vital service the cordgrass performs is to maintain the marsh channels. Since water moves more slowly over the grass-choked flats than in the free-flowing channels, it drops its sediment on the flats and the channels remain clear. Together the sediment and the decaying root systems form a thick, rich mulch that provides a superb growing ground for the plants the marsh inhabitants eat in order to survive.

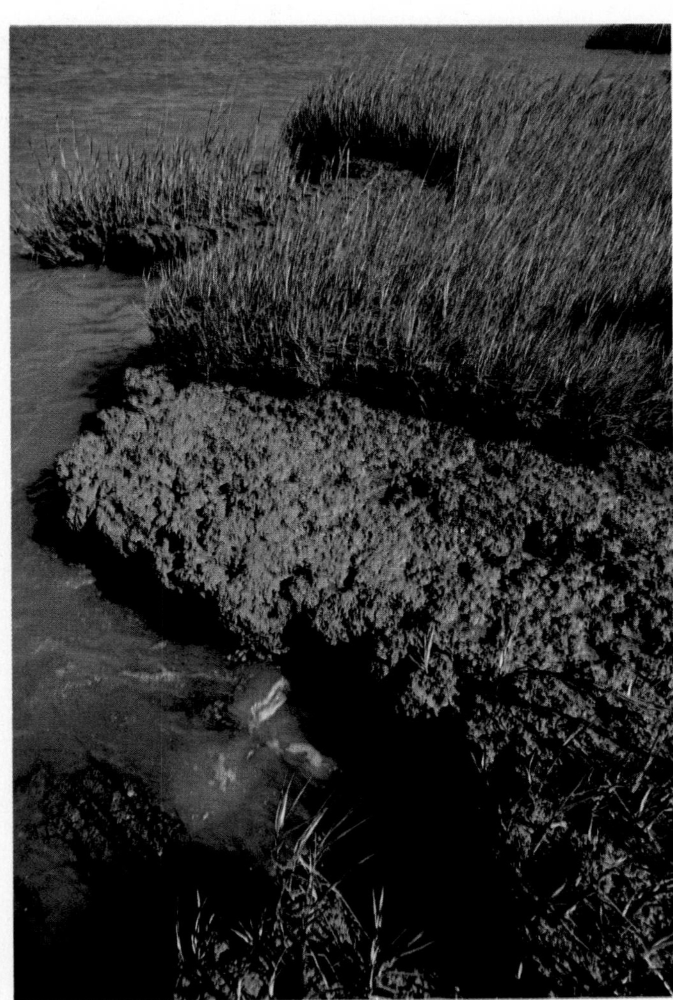

A CORDGRASS-TOPPED MUDBANK—LOW TIDE

Thriving Denizens of the Marshes

The creatures at right are but four of the hundreds of different species that prosper in the food-rich channels and flatlands of a salt marsh. The ultimate source of their food is cordgrass, as well as other plants that grow on the drier margins of the marsh. All told, the marsh produces an average of 7.3 tons of nutritious green matter per acre each year, a yield exceeding that of most tilled, fertilized farmland.

Food production in the marsh begins when the grass dies and is attacked by bacteria and fungi. These microscopic organisms break down the structure of the grass into particles tiny enough for other creatures to ingest, producing a thin soup made protein rich by the presence of the bacteria in it. This disintegrated material, or detritus, is eaten by the smaller marsh creatures, which in turn are eaten by larger ones.

While detritus is the diet staple of the four species pictured here, each has its own way of getting at the food. Oysters siphon water into their shells and extract the nutrients from it. Periwinkles shinny up and down cordgrass, munching on the film of bacteria and fungi covering the stalks. The fiddler crab and the billfish add to their diet of detritus by also feasting on smaller detritus-eating organisms. The billfish shown here, an infant 10 inches long, will fatten on detritus-nourished minnows before heading for the ocean and growing to a length of four feet.

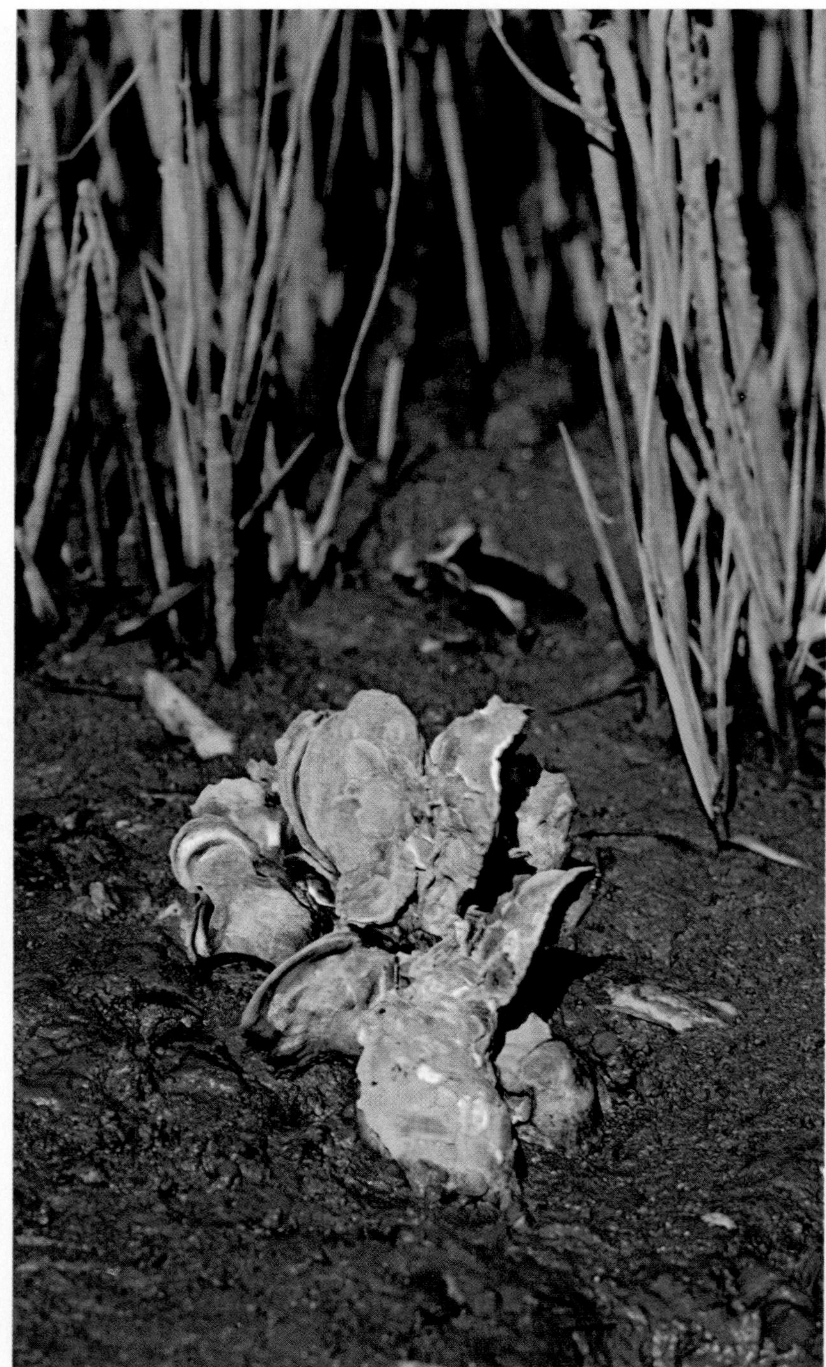

A CLUSTER OF OYSTERS ON A MUDBANK

CHANNEL SWIMMER: A BABY BILLFISH

SCUTTLING FIDDLER CRABS

MARSH PERIWINKLES CLIMBING CORDGRASS

Low vegetation and a stand of trees rise abruptly on the landward side of a marsh. The cordgrass in the foreground gives way, as the land

level rises, to plants that would perish if their roots were constantly in salt water—bayberry bushes, then cedar trees and loblolly pines.

6/ The Outer Banks

Today a little more land may belong to the sea, tomorrow a little less. Always the edge of the sea remains an elusive and indefinable boundary. RACHEL CARSON/ *THE EDGE OF THE SEA*

The first European explorers to approach the coast of North Carolina found a long, narrow strip of land with what looked like a limitless ocean behind it. In 1524 Giovanni da Verrazano, an Italian navigator in the service of the King of France, reported to his royal employer that he had discovered an isthmus separating the Atlantic from the Pacific. What he had actually found was North Carolina's Outer Banks. The body of water beyond was Pamlico Sound, so wide that the American mainland could not be seen.

Verrazano's error is understandable, for the Outer Banks are unique among barrier islands. Instead of hugging the coast, they curve out to sea sometimes as far as 30 miles to form an eastward-bulging chain that extends more than 175 miles from the Virginia border to Cape Lookout. A 90-mile-long highway serves the Outer Banks, but the road exists only by sufferance of the sea. Sometimes the waves charge over the dunes to attack the road; drifts of wind-blown sand build up on the blacktop. Trees and bushes that stand in the open are sculptured by salt spray into forms as rounded as boulders. The air smells of the sea, and the birds in the air are sea birds. Along much of this seagoing highway one gets the overwhelming impression that the ocean is waiting grimly for the proper moment to wash it away altogether.

How the Outer Banks came to be so far out in the ocean can only be surmised. One theory, advanced by Robert Dolan, professor of environmental sciences at the University of Virginia, is that the barrier islands were formed about 5,000 years ago by a confluence of longshore currents flowing south from Chesapeake Bay and offshore currents that piled up sand in amounts greater than normal. After the barriers were formed, the sea gradually flooded the coastal lowland behind them, a continuous process that created what is now Pamlico Sound and north of it Albemarle Sound. The waves and currents of the rising sea, aided by cooperative winds, shifted the sand of the barriers westward, but not as fast as the coastline was being flooded. The final result was the odd geography of North Carolina with its sheltering islands far out of sight of the mainland.

Toward the end of the 18th Century the Outer Banks had a scattering of English settlers in a few villages on the higher parts of the islands that were relatively safe from the sea. Some of these villages still exist and in places there are modern resort developments, but the greater part of the Outer Banks is uninhabited except for wildlife, especially snow geese and other waterfowl that winter there. Most of the Outer Banks' seemingly endless beaches, starting with a stretch on Bodie Island at the northern end of the chain and including nearly all those on Hatteras and Ocracoke Islands to the south, came under the protection of the federal government in 1953 as the first national seashore.

The highway threading the Outer Banks can be reached by two convenient routes. One connects the mainland to Bodie Island by a bridge across Currituck Sound, a narrow northern extension of Pamlico Sound. The other approach, farther south, is by a bridge from the mainland to Roanoke Island and by a causeway from there to Bodie Island.

I approached the Outer Banks by the more northerly route. The first village I came to on Bodie Island was Kitty Hawk, where Orville and Wilbur Wright flew the first successful airplane in 1903. From Kitty Hawk to Nags Head, the southernmost community on Bodie Island, the scenery has been everywhere devastated by man. No native trees or bushes remain, and those that have been recently planted are sickly and unprotected from the wind. Even the usually hardy beach grass grows in feeble patches, and without its stabilizing roots the yellow sand advances in small billows between seaside stores and cottages.

But a few miles south of Nags Head, where the Outer Banks begin their widest swing out to sea and a sign announces "Cape Hatteras National Seashore," the prospect abruptly changes. Weeds grow beside the road, and healthy dunes covered with thriving beach grass fill the space between road and beach. Sea oats, their plumelike golden seed heads swaying gently atop long graceful stems, ornament the dunes, and on the sheltered slopes rounded bayberry bushes huddle in clusters. Here and there young cedar trees raise their feathery branches into the salty breeze. From this point southward to the national seashore's end on Ocracoke Island, nature and man have collaborated to create that strange, wild beauty—part sea, part land—that can be found only on the Outer Banks.

Although the 15- to 20-foot-high dunes that rise behind the beach for most of the national seashore's length appear natural, they are not entirely so. They have been stabilized with the help of piled-up barriers of brush to collect blowing sand and let beach grass get a roothold. Much of this work was done during the Great Depression of the 1930s by the Civilian Conservation Corps and other agencies. As the dunes grew, posts or snow fencing were sometimes added to encourage them to grow higher. For long stretches this dune line permits only sporadic views of the ocean from the Outer Banks highway, and the traveler mostly sees placid Pamlico Sound and a strip of salt marsh to the west. But the dunes just as effectively screen the road from the beach. When you venture out on the beach from one of the turnouts provided by the Park Service, the highway might as well never have been built. Though it is well traveled, beyond the dunes it cannot be seen, smelled or heard. In early September, when I was last there, I walked for miles without encountering a trace of human existence other than a few bits of flotsam. In majesty and solitude the great Atlantic swells break on offshore sandbars or crash high up on the beach.

As I traveled southward on Hatteras Island—largest of the Outer Banks—and on Ocracoke Island, the many stretches of beach I tramped were wonderfully deserted. In places where the full force of the waves was spent offshore, the beach was wide, smooth and made of fine tan-colored sand mixed with coarser fragments of wave-polished shells. There was plenty of room for the shore birds patrolling the swash line for food, among them thin-legged willets and ruddy turnstones with bold plumage in black, white and rusty red. The stocky ruddy turnstones were the busiest birds of all as they investigated every crack in the sand and—living up to their names—tipped over pebbles and pieces of shell in their quest for tidbits. On the upper reaches of the beach an occasional hardy plant pioneer, such as sprawling beach spurge or sea rocket—so called for its bullet-shaped seed capsules—had succeeded in establishing itself. Behind the sparse pioneers, beach grass was spreading out from the dunes, collecting sand and advancing the edge of the land toward the ocean. In other places a strikingly different scene offered graphic evidence that the Outer Banks are still changing in response to natural forces as they have done for thousands of years. Here it was the sea that was advancing. The beach was narrow. The waves were breaking directly against the dunes, making the sand slump into their foam and leaving steep banks festooned with trailing grass roots. Left to itself in such places, the sea would probably cut an inlet through the narrow land to Pamlico Sound.

So many inlets have opened and closed in the Outer Banks that it is difficult to keep track of them. Some low and narrow sections of the Outer Banks are, in fact, "inlet prone." Almost any violent storm blowing from the proper direction may cut an opening—which can close in a few months or remain open for years. Sir Walter Raleigh's "lost colony" on Roanoke Island, founded in 1585 and the first English settlement in the New World, was given access to the sea by broad, deep Roanoke Inlet—long since filled in and now part of Bodie Island.

Other sections of the Outer Banks have proved less vulnerable to the eroding power of the sea, and have collected enough sand to form substantial hills. The southern end of Hatteras Island boasts a hill rising 50 feet above sea level, and a considerable area near the hill is also fairly high and covered with a flourishing forest known as Buxton Woods.

Buxton Woods is the largest and tallest stand of trees on the Outer Banks. It occupies about 3,000 acres, a third of them within the boundaries of the national seashore. Like the Sunken Forest on Fire Island off Long Island's south shore, it grows on the crests and slopes of old dunes. Filling many of the valleylike depressions between the dune ridges of Buxton Woods are shrub thickets, vine jungles, marshy spots and fresh-water ponds. Among the dominant trees are loblolly pines up to 30 feet tall, ironwood, holly, dogwood and live oak, the hardest and staunchest of all oaks and formerly valued as bracing for wooden sailing ships. Also common are dwarf palmettos, among the northernmost wild palms of the Atlantic coast, with fronds that rise directly out of the ground without a supporting trunk. Between the dunes some of the thickets, as impenetrable as any I have seen, consist largely of a plant with the curious name of devil's-walking-stick or Hercules'-club. As I followed the trail that threads the national seashore section of Buxton Woods, I remembered my futile attempt to force my way through a bullbrier tangle on Fire Island and took care not to stray from the path to try to challenge the forbidding thickets of devil's-walking-stick; its long,

straight stems, armed with vicious spines over half an inch long, were distinctly uninviting.

One of the hollies that grows liberally in Buxton Woods is a southern variety called yaupon, a large, attractive shrub with very light gray bark, clusters of brilliant red berries in winter—and an interesting history. The coastal Indians used its small caffein-yielding leaves to brew a "black drink" that was so popular other Indians came from miles inland to enjoy it. Later the European colonists developed a taste for the aromatic, pleasant-tasting drink; a mid-18th Century writer reported that it was "as much in use among the white people as among the Indians, at least among those who inhabit the sea-coasts." Exporting the dried, slightly scalloped leaves of yaupon, which thrives not only in Buxton Woods but throughout much of the Outer Banks, became an industry on the islands. When Union ships blockaded Southern ports during the Civil War and there were no incoming cargoes of coffee or tea, yaupon "tea" was widely used as a substitute in the South; it became a habit, and is still drunk on the Outer Banks.

Along the open beach and among the grass-covered dunes I had not noticed much wildlife. Most of it consisted of shore birds and gulls and, on the higher reaches of the beach, a few ghost crabs; once in a while an eight-inch lizard with a long, whiplike tail—called a six-lined race runner for the half dozen whitish stripes down its back—darted across my path. But in Buxton Woods the wildlife is considerably more varied. The combination of dense cover, marsh and fresh-water ponds provides homes for all manner of creatures, a few of them best avoided; one sign on the trail warns: "A snake you see here may be a deadly cottonmouth." I met no poisonous snakes myself, only a harmless, blunt-headed hognose snake sunning itself at the forest's edge. It did not turn belly up and play dead as a surprised hognose commonly does, but quickly vanished into a thicket at my approach.

Though the woods contain mammals ranging in size from white-tailed deer to delicate little white-footed deer mice—the smallest of North American mice—they are either nocturnal prowlers or stay well concealed in the thick underbrush. The chances of observing wildlife are better around the comparatively open marshes and ponds cradled between the wooded dunes. From November to March such places are crowded with migratory waterfowl; most of the year the more open areas are well-stocked hunting grounds for mink, otter, muskrat and raccoon, which feed on the abundance of small fish, snails, frogs and other aquatic creatures.

At Cape Hatteras, tasseled ears of sea oats decorate the border of Pamlico Sound. These reeds sometimes grow almost as tall as a man.

Among the turtles that find cozy homes in the muddy banks of ponds and marshes is the celebrated diamondback terrapin, whose succulent flesh is much sought by gourmets for making savory soups and stews. I saw several terrapin resting motionless in the sun on a half-submerged log, their carapaces distinctively marked with concentric patterns that vaguely suggested diamonds. It was hard to imagine these lethargic sun bathers as great travelers, but in early summer the females leave the mudbanks to find nesting places on drier land and sometimes lumber as much as half a mile before finding a satisfactory site in which to dig a hole and deposit their eggs. About an inch long, the newly hatched diamondbacks that are not gobbled up by predators—raccoons and foxes—en route find their way by instinct back to the moisture and security of the ponds and marshland.

Late one afternoon on the edge of a pond fringed with stands of cattails and the bright green stalks of wild rice, I saw what at first glance looked like a beaver. It was nearly a yard long with reddish-brown fur, and as it moved about complacently feeding on water plants I noticed that, like a beaver's, its hind feet were webbed, but that it lacked the beaver's flat, paddlelike tail. I later described this puzzling animal to a shopkeeper in the nearby village of Hatteras, one of the 700 or so people who live there year round. He informed me that I had been watching a nutria. These large rodents, native to South America and said to be good eating as well as commercially useful for their fur, were introduced to the Outer Banks about 30 years ago by a gun club. Being prolific breeders, they soon spread widely through Hatteras Island, where they are known as Russian rats.

The coiners of that epithet—the natives of the Outer Banks, generally called Bankers—are as unusual as the islands themselves. The first few permanent English settlers, who arrived in the mid-17th Century, lived simultaneously as farmers, fishermen, hunters and wreckers. They got along fine with the aborigines, the friendly and peaceful Croatoan Indians, and apparently intermarried with them, for one early account tells of "Indians with grey eyes." By the late 1600s, wealthy mainland landowners were using the narrow Outer Banks, which needed no confining fences, for breeding cattle, horses, sheep and hogs. Most of the inhabitants, however, were squatters and fugitives—some of them described as "Pyrats and runaway Servants"—and people who for some other reason valued the extreme isolation that the Outer Banks provided. They seldom went to the mainland. They fished, gathered shellfish, hunted ducks and geese in the salt marshes, cultivated plots of corn and other vegetables, and kept an eye on the beaches for stranded whales and any useful wreckage that might come ashore.

In the mid-18th Century an official of the royal colony of North Carolina described the Bankers as "a set of people . . . who are very Wild and ungovernable, so that it is seldom possible to Execute any Civil or Criminal Writs among them." Activities on the Outer Banks during the early years of that century helped to establish the Bankers' reputation for wildness. Pirates lurked in the inlets and hidden coves and terrorized coastal shipping. The most infamous was Blackbeard (Edward Teach), who worked in league with the Governor of North Carolina and sailed out of Ocracoke, where a deep channel is still known as Teach's Hole. This did not upset the North Carolinians unduly as long as Blackbeard limited his attacks to offshore shipping, but when he also captured small local vessels they turned to the Governor of Virginia for help. Late in 1718 two sloops of the Royal Navy arrived at Ocracoke, attacked the pirate flagship, and engaged it in a bloody battle. Blackbeard was killed. The commander of one of the sloops then sailed up the Pamlico River to the North Carolina town of Bath with the pirate's head dangling from the bowsprit. With Blackbeard's death, the great era of piracy on the Outer Banks came to an end.

The first settlers came to the Outer Banks in late Elizabethan times —a century before Blackbeard's death. Occasionally their descendants will still come out with an expression handed down from that distant era. Asked if he drank his yaupon tea with sugar, cream or lemon, an old man told a friend of mine he preferred to take his tea "reverent." Puzzled, my friend later looked up this variant of a familiar word and found that in the days of the first Elizabeth "reverent" had meant "pure"; in short, the old fellow liked his yaupon straight. Even today most native Bankers have not acquired the soft Southern accent of most North Carolinians. To me their speech sounded more like a variant of New England English. I asked one sea-weathered old Banker to explain this. "A lot of our granddaddies was washed ashore," he said matter-of-factly, "and mostly from Northern ships. So why should we talk Southern?" There was a twinkle in his eye to show that he did not expect his explanation to be taken literally, but wrecks were indeed commonplace in the islands in the age of sail and the early years of steamboating. With their violent storms and treacherous shoals, the Outer Banks were notorious as the graveyard of the Atlantic. Once in a great while, on the long, lonely beaches, a gaunt skeleton of an old ship, the ribs bristling with rusty iron fastenings, may be found sticking up out of the sand.

Modern navigation aids and an efficient storm-warning system have almost ended such catastrophes as shipwrecks, but the fury of the ocean is as powerful and menacing as ever. No one listens for storm warnings more carefully than the Bankers. Their islands, reaching far into the ocean, stand in the path of many Caribbean-born hurricanes; moreover, winter nor'easters that prove of minor effect elsewhere may cause serious damage here, either by direct assault or by backing water up in Pamlico Sound that later spills out over the islands. All Bankers remember with awe the Ash Wednesday storm of 1962 and the havoc created as waves washed over parts of the Outer Banks and in some places drove the shoreline more than 200 feet inland. A new inlet, since filled, was cut completely across Hatteras Island, and a temporary bridge was built to connect the Outer Banks highway, sections of which had to be abandoned and rebuilt farther from the sea.

The focal point of the ocean's violence is around Cape Hatteras, which stands where Hatteras Island angles sharply westward. It is the jutting elbow of the Outer Banks, thrust out against the brunt of the Atlantic's summer hurricanes. The beach is broad and flat. There are no trees to bend with the wind, no buildings or jetties or hills to oppose and channel the hurricane's fury.

Not many people venture out onto Cape Hatteras when a hurricane flails it. Most Bankers ride out a storm indoors, close to a radio, occasionally going to a window to check the tide. But a hardy few are drawn to the storm-lashed beaches by the challenge of confronting the elements in their wildest state.

I talked with one Hatteras resident who had walked on the Cape during a recent hurricane. He said the air was like a moving wall, made thick and almost impenetrable by gusts of 100 miles per hour or more. To walk he had to lean into the gale as if against the push of a giant hand, vainly trying to avoid the sand and water the wind hurled at him. Turning around or changing direction became a delicate balancing act as the gusts veered capriciously, sometimes catching him sideways and knocking him down. Trying to get up, he found that the sand, windblown into thick masses at ground level, had bitten into the flesh of his hands with the abrasive force of a rasp.

Huge waves crashed onto the beach and gnawed at the dunes where beach grass and reeds were bent flat, clinging to the sand by their roots. Between waves, the wind, defying gravity, pushed the water up the

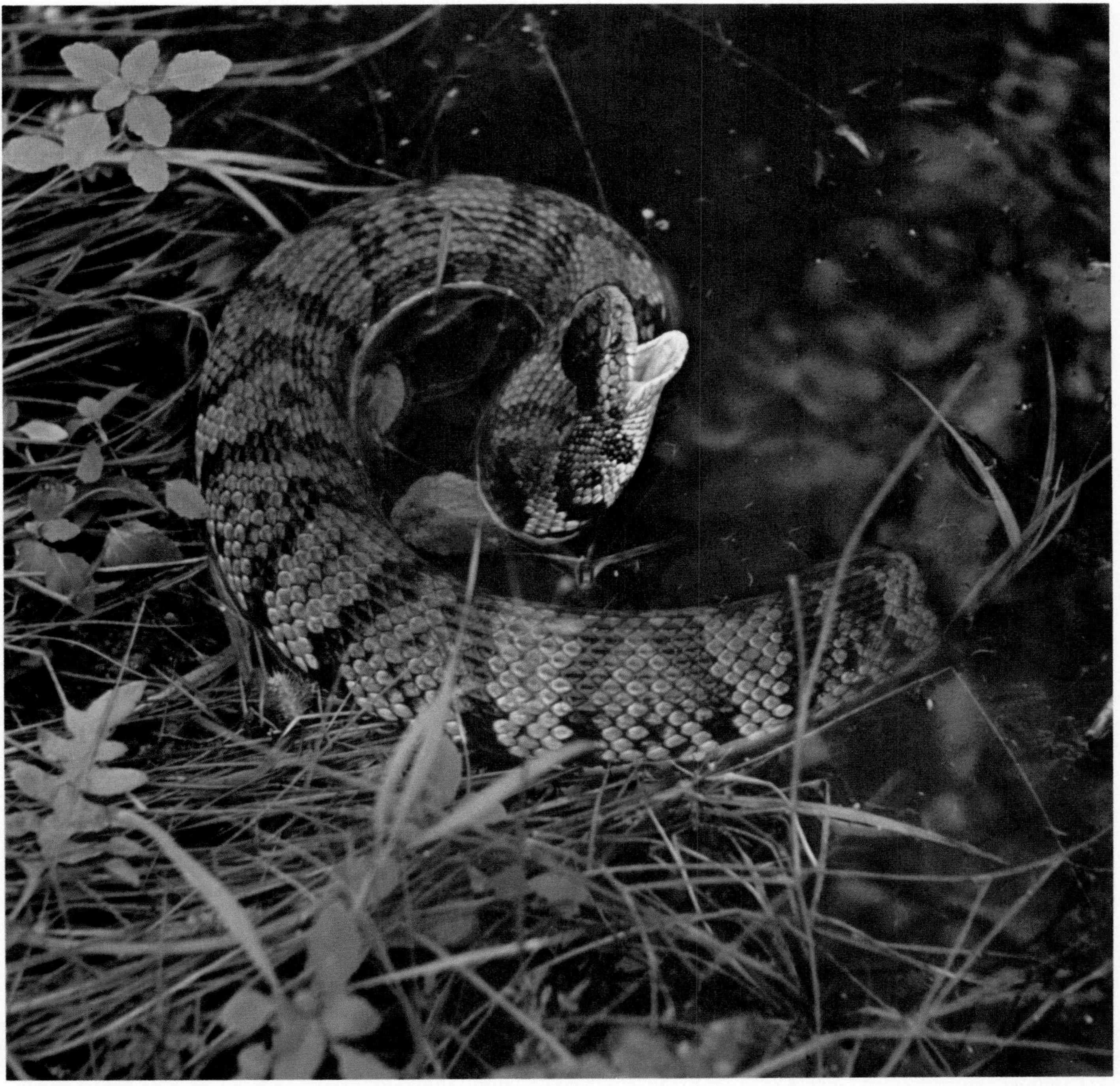

Identifiable by its black and gold bands, a poisonous cottonmouth lies half submerged in a shady woodland pool on Cape Hatteras.

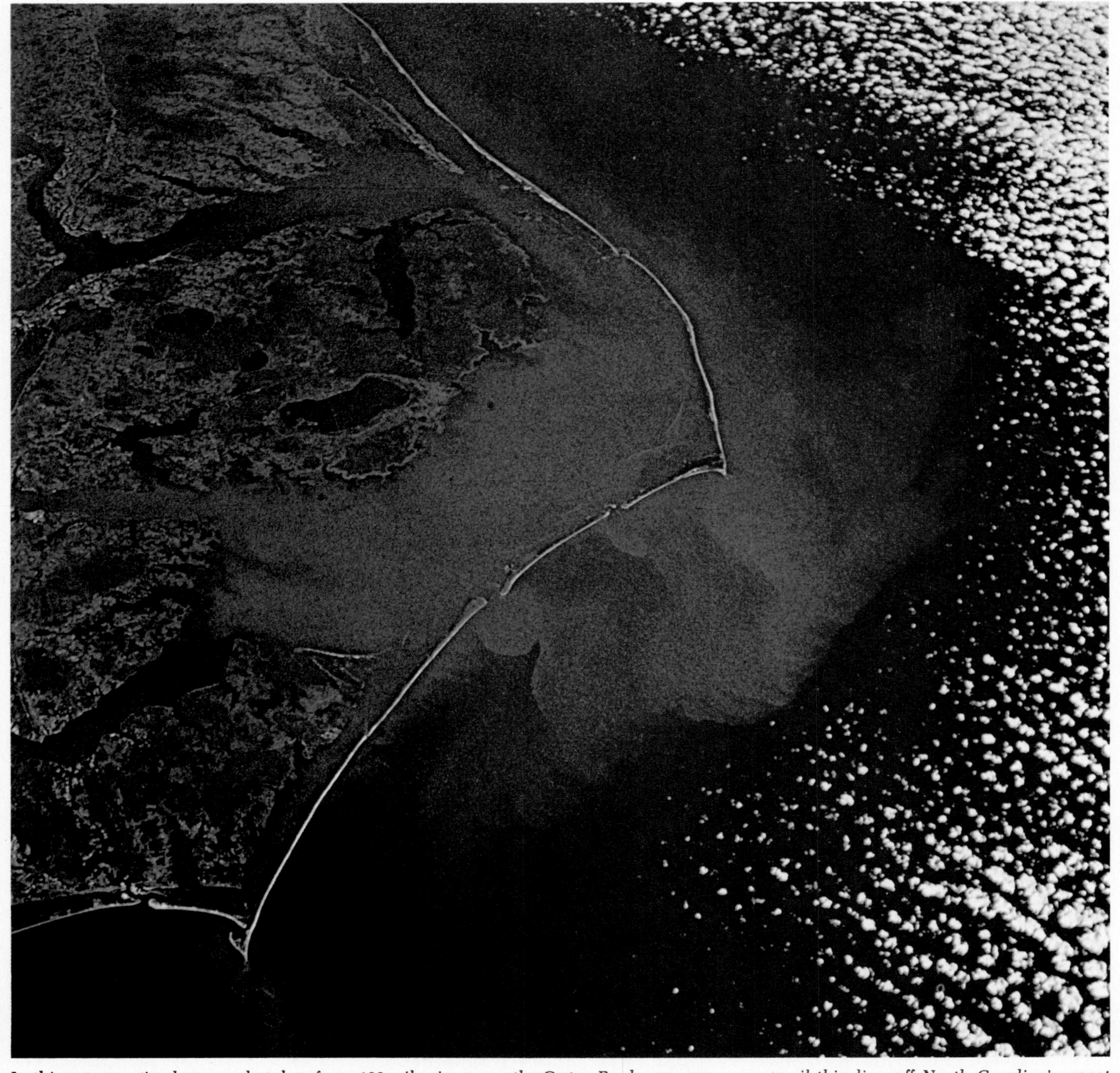

In this astronaut's photograph, taken from 120 miles in space, the Outer Banks appear as a pencil-thin line off North Carolina's coast.

beach in great fan-shaped sheets. The water whipped itself at its edges into a white froth that broke apart in sudsy fragments and tumbled crazily toward the dunes.

Although well bundled in foul-weather gear, my venturesome acquaintance was soon soaked to the skin, which chafed with sand that had penetrated inside his clothes. Finally the wind began to affect him with a sense of almost palpable malevolence, he said, and when the backwash of a particularly powerful wave almost pulled him into the surf he decided to call it quits. Although he didn't say so, I got the distinct impression that the experience had shaken him, and that the next hurricane to assault the Cape would find him safely indoors.

The Cape, with its lighthouse towering more than 200 feet—the tallest in North America—is a dramatic place. Especially spectacular is the narrow sandspit that runs out to sea beyond the lighthouse. I was lucky enough to see it during a violent gale, and incidentally to get a firsthand idea of what my Hatteras friend was talking about. The waves on the main beach were tremendous, and out beyond the tip of the spit I could see enormous spouts of foam that looked like products of underwater explosions. After making sure that the tide was ebbing, I walked out on the spit, which was perhaps two miles long and a hundred yards across. Great waves were breaking diagonally on the windward side, and on the leeward side smaller waves were moving against the wind to break in a smaller line of surf. The wind was at my back and was strong enough to propel me toward the tip of the spit like a sailing ship running free.

The spouts of foam came nearer and grew higher. Now I could see that they were caused by waves from opposite directions colliding off the tip of the spit and tossing their foamy water high in the air. For a long time I watched this wild commotion, feeling as far from land as if I were in mid-ocean.

Fighting the wind on my way back to the shore, I had an experience unique in all my years of beach walking. I was blown down. I was wearing a sou'wester and was pushing into the stinging sand and spray with lowered head, trying to watch my footing. During an especially violent gust I put my foot forward and found nothing solid to set it on. It felt like stepping into a deep hole. The next thing I knew I was on my back looking up at low clouds scudding overhead. I was not at all hurt, but whenever I hear or read the expression "Blow me down!" I think of my walk on that sandspit.

The Cape Hatteras National Seashore and seagoing highway end with Ocracoke Island, whose main village has become attractive enough to visitors to contain two restaurants and a few motels. But the Outer Banks continue southwestward for nearly 60 miles, approaching closer to the mainland and turning an abrupt corner to the west just before reaching Cape Lookout. This great stretch, most of which is known as Core Banks, has no permanent inhabitants except for Coast Guardsmen at Cape Lookout; it is in the process of being organized into the Cape Lookout National Seashore.

Since no road leads from Ocracoke Island to Core Banks, I returned to the mainland and hired a small private ferry (capable of carrying one automobile) and a man who agreed to take me anywhere I wanted to go on the longest island of Core Banks. The distance across Core Sound is only about five miles, but the Outer Banks are so low that the only part visible at first was a hummock off to the right that turned out to be a grove of small oaks and pines. The beach across the island was the loneliest I have ever seen. Wide and flat, it was made of fine sand covered in many places with broken shell fragments. There were no tracks on it, no signs of human life. The low-lying land behind it was just as lonely, with only a scattering of vegetation—yaupon shrubs and bayberry bushes. The only living creatures in sight were five or six large brown pelicans flapping by in line formation a dozen or so feet above the surf. I have seen pelicans elsewhere amid less desolate surroundings (they occur as far north as Chesapeake Bay) and in those places they seemed merely grotesque. Perched on piers and hopefully awaiting handouts from fishermen, they shift clumsily from one broad webbed foot to another and waggle their enormous scooplike bills. Often when they dive into the sea for one of the surface-swimming fish that are their principal food, they hit the water in an ungainly belly whopper—perhaps with the idea of stunning their prey. But here on this lonely, barren beach they seemed eerie rather than comic, like creatures out of the distant past. They made me think of leathery-winged pterodactyls gliding above a manless world.

Core Banks were not always as bald and lonely as they are today. They once had forests in many places and villages of fishermen and shore whalers. Most of the villages were small and lasted only a short time, though one of them survived until very recently: Portsmouth, at the northern end of the Banks, a village laid out on Ocracoke Inlet in the 18th Century to house pilots who guided ships through the tricky inlet.

By 1850 Portsmouth's population had reached about 500, but in 1846 the sea had opened Hatteras Inlet, a deeper, wider channel 14 miles north. Shipping was diverted, and the village of Portsmouth slowly declined. Its last year-round inhabitant died in 1970. Diamond City, another community near Cape Lookout, also had something like 500 people when an 1899 hurricane flooded the town. In the next few years the people evacuated, many of them moving their houses to safer places on the mainland.

During their inhabited period, Core Banks and the short section to the west of Cape Lookout known as Shackleford Banks suffered grievously. Timber and firewood cutting destroyed most of the woods. Overgrazing by livestock largely denuded the land of stabilizing grasses and bushes, leaving the sand loose and blowing. Hills that were once up to 60 feet high near the southern end of Core Banks completely disappeared, and long stretches of the Outer Banks became so low that storms washed over them.

Today, Core and neighboring Shackleford Banks are reverting to wilderness once more—a clean slate on which the National Park Service can work to create a large and spectacularly beautiful national seashore that would be roadless and accessible only by ferry. The endless clean wide beaches are washed by warm water most of the year. With careful encouragement vegetation will return, starting with the humble beach grasses that catch sand and start dunes growing. The few remaining patches of forest will spread. Perhaps some day, if man and nature continue to cooperate, the 60-foot sandhills will rise again.

Lords of the Atlantic Flyway

Of the four major aerial corridors used by North American migratory birds, the Atlantic flyway is the longest, stretching 5,000 miles from the Arctic Ocean to the West Indies. On the flyway, the most numerous—and among the most spectacular—migrants are the hundreds of thousands of geese and ducks that spend the winter in some 30 wetland refuges along the coast from Massachusetts to North Carolina.

The Atlantic flyway resembles a funnel, with its wide end encompassing the region from central Alaska to the west coast of Greenland, and its neck extending along the Atlantic coast. Thus the geese that meet to spend the winter at Pea Island, North Carolina, may have flown there from such widely separated points in Canada as the eastern shore of Hudson Bay and the Labrador coast, 1,000 miles apart. It is in these far-flung northern areas that the birds breed.

Waterfowl start arriving in the Atlantic wintering grounds in September. When south-flying birds hit nor'-easters, they seek shelter; as the storm clears the congregated flocks take off together and wave after wave will alight on the wetlands. The birds usually segregate themselves by species and then crowd together. Canada geese sometimes assemble in huge groups called rafts that may include as many as 30,000 birds. The ducks are somewhat less fussy; the species frequently mingle with one another, and the flocks of ducks are always relatively small and inconspicuous.

Besides resting, the chief business of the birds in the wintering areas is eating, and the Atlantic wetlands offer the broad range of foods needed to supply species with very different feeding habits. Snow geese, for instance, are vegetarians, while Canada geese mix small crustaceans and insect larvae into their plant diet. Brant, small dainty geese, prefer bottom-growing eelgrass but will eat sea lettuce, a kind of seaweed. Among the ducks, the mallard, American widgeon and pintail prefer grass, plant roots and grain, but their diet includes about 15 per cent animal food. Eider ducks eat almost nothing but mussels and crustaceans. To help their gizzards grind up the shells, the birds require large amounts of gravel—small pebbles may account for up to 15 per cent of the contents of their digestive tracts —and that substance, too, is available in quantity in the wetlands.

Four greater snow geese–identifiable by their gleaming white plumage and black-tipped wings–brake for a landing on the salt marshes of Pea Island, North Carolina, the southern terminus of their fall migration.

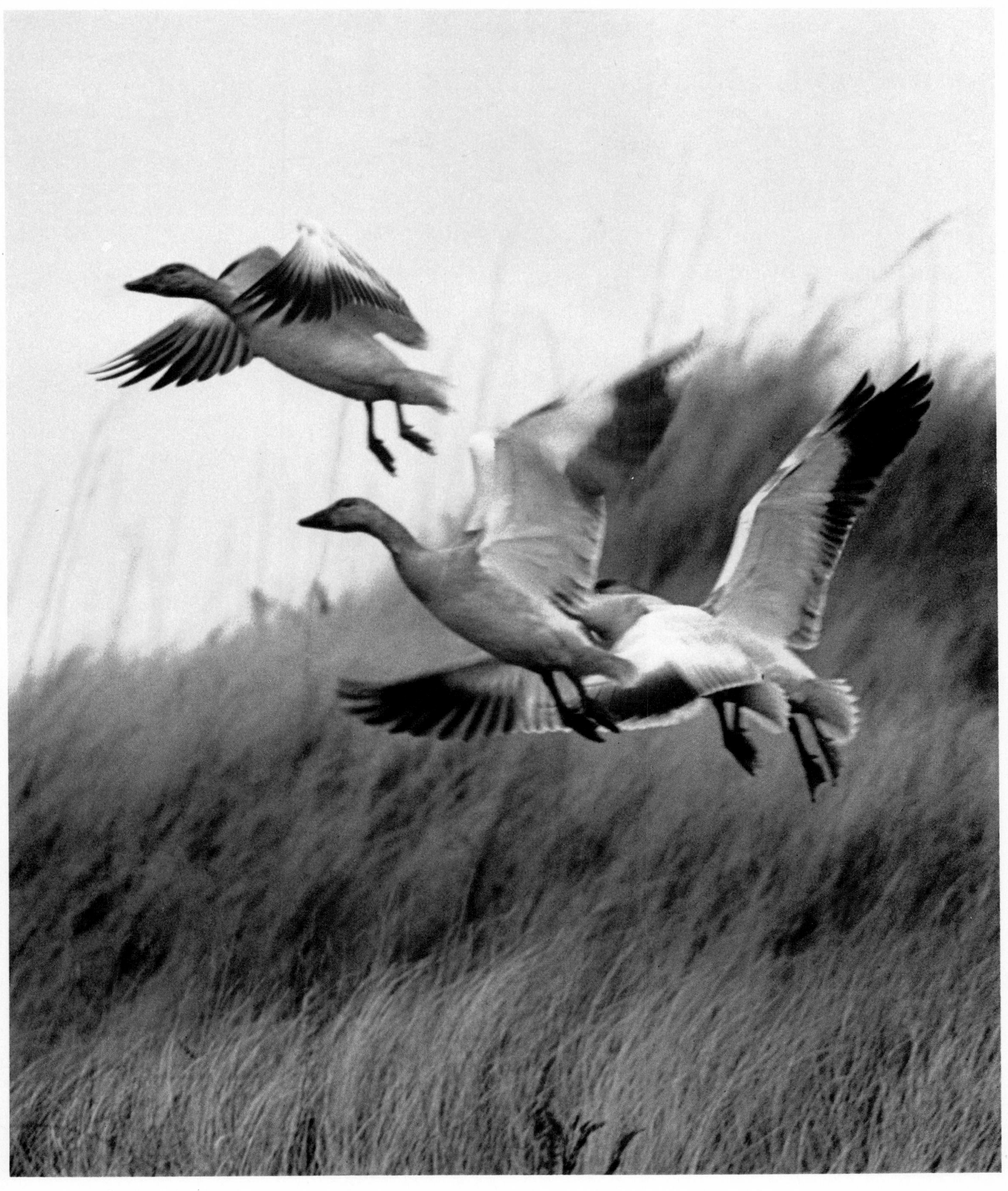

The Geese—Harvesters of the Marsh

Family-conscious birds that mate for life, geese spend the winter in the Atlantic wetlands along the flyway carefully nurturing their young. The greater snow geese in the photograph at right are shown in their characteristic guardian role—watching the horizon for danger while the goslings, distinguished by their gray plumage, gorge safely on the stems and bulbous roots of marsh grass and rushes.

When feeding, geese of all ages and types use their long necks to drive their bills into the mud and break off the plants with a twist of the head and a jerk of the neck. They can expel marsh water from their mouths without losing the food, which is retained in their broad bills by an arrangement of overlapping toothlike serrations.

Like an army of harvesters, greater snow geese, flocking to the wetlands by the hundreds of thousands, can strip huge areas of marsh of vegetation. In their passage they churn up the mud with their feet and bills, and tracts of wetlands worked over by wintering geese often resemble hog wallows.

But the mess they make is usually temporary. After the geese migrate northward in the spring, the marsh heals itself, replacing the harvest with new growth over the summer. When the great flocks return to their wintering grounds with the first snap of cold weather, their food supply will have been replenished.

SNOW GEESE ON ASSATEAGUE ISLAND, MARYLAND

In the glow of a November sunset, a flock of Canada geese, honkers famed for their precise V-shaped flight formation, settle in (left) for the night on the marshlands of Blackwater National Wildlife Refuge, Maryland. This brownish-gray bird, with its long black neck and prominent white cheek patches, is the largest of the geese—weighing up to 14 pounds and often attaining a maximum wingspread of nearly six feet. As many as 80,000 of this species winter at Blackwater.

Not a migrant but a permanent resident of the Brigantine Refuge in southern New Jersey, a Canada goose sits on a nest built of marsh reeds. All but a few Canada geese nest in the far north; this bird is descended from geese that had their wings clipped to prevent them from flying in the spring to their habitual breeding grounds. Hatched at the refuge, their young remained year round, creating a unique flock of 600 Canada geese that have given up the strenuous migratory life.

PINTAIL DRAKE

AMERICAN-WIDGEON DRAKE

AMERICAN-EIDER HEN

The Ducks—Colorful and Diverse

Among the 22 species of ducks that use the Middle Atlantic section of the flyway are four that display a particularly striking diversity of size, coloration and habits.

The green-headed mallard *(right)*, ancestor of most domestic breeds, is the most numerous duck on the flyway; in peak years over 750,000 winter in the Atlantic refuges and wetlands. Typical of surface-feeding ducks, mallards prefer shallow waters, where they are voracious destroyers of mosquito larvae.

Another shallow-water feeder, the handsome, sleek pintail *(top left)* has a coppery head and an elongated tail. Pintails are among the swiftest and most powerful fliers of the duck family, clocked by pilots at speeds up to 65 miles per hour.

Another speedy duck is the cream-and-brown American widgeon *(center left)*, nicknamed the baldpate for its white forehead and crown. Its most notable characteristic is its habit of stealing from its neighbors, including such species as the canvasback, which feed by diving. As the diver surfaces, a baldpate may attack it and snatch fronds of pondgrass from its bill.

The champion diver, unworried by the vegetarian baldpate, is the shellfish-eating brown-and-white barred American eider *(bottom left)*. Seldom seen out of water, the eider, using its wings to help it swim, can dive as deep as 60 feet to harvest the mollusks that are its favored diet.

A PAIR OF MALLARDS–DRAKE AND HEN

Silhouetted against a spring moon, a flock of American brant, dark geese so small they are often mistaken for ducks, head north from

Brigantine, New Jersey. In flight, brant move in disorderly patterns that contrast with the disciplined flight formations of other geese.

7/ Winter Bird Havens

All suddenly mount/ And scatter wheeling in great broken rings/ Upon their clamorous wings.

WILLIAM BUTLER YEATS/ *THE WILD SWANS AT COOLE*

Along the Eastern seaboard of the United States there is a heavily traveled route, studded with rest stops and eating places, that meets with the full approval of conservationists. The major travelers on this fascinating artery are water birds, and the rest stops and eating places are primarily theirs, to replenish themselves in their autumn migrations south and spring migrations back north again. Different species use the Atlantic flyway in different ways. Some birds spend the winter in bays and estuaries on the Middle Atlantic coast. Others follow the flyway southward at leisure, pausing often on marshes, beaches and tidal lagoons to rest and feed. Still others stop only to cram their stomachs with food for long overwater flights to destinations in the Southern Hemisphere. Years ago the water birds came in flocks so huge they reportedly darkened the sky. They still come in numbers that are an inspiration to see.

Among the beneficiaries of the flyway were the Pilgrim Fathers. Edward Winslow described the October preparations for the first Thanksgiving as follows: "Our harvest being gotten in, our Governor sent four men on fowling. . . . The four in one day killed as much fowl as, with a little help beside, served the Company almost a week." Those fowl were most likely migrating ducks and geese. The wild turkeys usually linked with Thanksgiving were too scarce and wary to be collected quickly in such quantity.

The numbers of water birds have been much diminished by hunting and pollution—and above all by the pressure of human population. But only three species, the Eskimo curlew, the Labrador duck and the great auk, have been exterminated; there is even some doubt about the curlew's fate, and several species that were endangered are making healthy comebacks. A principal reason for this upturn is the chain of wildlife refuges that has been established along the flyway, where the birds are safe from hunters during the open season and where their natural feeding grounds are protected and sometimes improved. Many such sanctuaries are small and out of the way; others are relatively large and accessible. Often during my exploration of beaches and marshes I have been delighted to come on great congregations of secure and sassy birds: many kinds of cheerful little ducks, stately whistling swans, burly Canada geese, snow geese from the Arctic and graceful shore birds. Well do they know they are safe in the refuges.

There are millions of hunters and men who think of themselves as hunters, and they are supported by a politically powerful industry that lives by supplying them with guns and other costly apparatus. So there will always be places and seasons for killing water birds. But an ever-increasing number of people merely want to look at birds, to admire their beauty and the grace of their flight. It is likely that the refuges will increase in number and improve in management of land and wildlife. Even some of the worst-polluted marshes can be cleaned up enough for migrant birds to use as flyway feeding grounds as they did in the time of the Pilgrims.

One of the Atlantic flyway refuges, Monomoy Island, is a much better place for birds today than it was a hundred years ago. Monomoy was once a narrow sandy peninsula jutting southward toward Nantucket from the "elbow" of Cape Cod. It had a small fishing village on its tip with a road of sorts leading to it and was a favorite place for market hunters, who lay in wait for great flocks of migrating plovers, ducks and geese, which they killed by the barrelful to sell in Boston or New York. Some of the more vulnerable species were almost wiped out before federal laws and treaties with Canada began to outlaw commercial hunting and put amateur hunters under increasing regulation. Two additional strokes of good fortune for the birds of Monomoy were the abandonment of the fishing village when its harbor filled up with sand, and a storm that broke a mile-wide channel through the northern end of the peninsula, creating an island eight miles long and, in places, one and a half miles wide.

Most of the time the birds have Monomoy to themselves. Thousands of terns—"mackerel gulls" as Cape Codders call them—nest on the upper beach or among the beach grass. Black ducks and green-winged teal nest on strips of marsh between sandy ridges in the interior of the island and feed in the fresh- or salt-water ponds. Shore birds of many kinds play tag with the foaming surf or feed on the broad mud flats exposed at low tide. They have nothing to fear from man, for the island is now a national wildlife refuge area barred to hunters.

Monomoy becomes a busy station on the Atlantic flyway in late summer as shore birds that have nested in the Arctic—some of them as far north as land may be found—are driven south by the threat of winter. Quick-moving plovers with their stubby bills, crowd-loving dowitchers, soft-honking knots and many kinds of sandpipers settle down on Monomoy to renew the stores of fat they use as flying fuel. After resting and feeding for a few days on the worms, crustaceans and other small marine creatures with which the island's muddy flats abound, they take off once again over the ocean. Some may not touch land again until they reach South America.

After the shore birds have gone, the ducks and geese arrive at Monomoy. The most spectacular are the Canada geese, flying high in perfect "V" formations and uttering their haunting cries, which can be heard for miles. I have often wondered how many modern Americans have ever thrilled to this sound. In the New York City suburb where I live now, I have seen many flocks of geese fly over. They can be plainly heard between the roar of passing autos, but few people glance up.

Canada geese always look as if they know precisely where they are going, even when they are headed in the wrong direction. Late one October on Cape Cod I went to call on a well-known ornithologist. On the way to meet him I saw a magnificent "V" formation of geese flying due north toward the oncoming ice and snow. I asked the ornithologist what he thought they were doing. He repeated a story about them that is interesting, if questionable: that they were descendants of the live decoys that hunters formerly tethered in ponds to lure their wild fellows down to death. When live decoys were made illegal, some of the birds were released. Their progeny, which are year-round residents of Cape Cod, feel vaguely that they ought to migrate somewhere in fall but have no clear idea of where they should go. As likely as not, however, the northward-flying geese were simply making a short local flight from one feeding ground to another.

Ducks do not fly in purposeful "V"s. They migrate in disorganized flocks, stopping often, like tourists with plenty of time on their hands, to rest and sample the food here and there. In my opinion the most interesting ducks are the eiders, which breed on the hostile coast of Labrador and insulate their nests with fluffy down plucked from their breasts. Eiders know enough to follow the coast in a generally southerly direction about half a mile offshore, but when they come to Cape Cod they are sometimes baffled by its hooked shape, turn north, then realize something is wrong. The flocks break up and mill in confusion, and some make several circuits of the Cape before the more observant birds see open water on its far side and head south to Monomoy and Nantucket Sound. There they spend the winter on the water, sometimes as many as 50,000 of them, tossing on the icy waves and never coming ashore except if injured—or soaked by some ship's oil spill.

Eiders feed by diving down to the great beds of mussels that pave the shallow parts of the sea bottom. An eider no bigger than a chicken can swallow a mussel more than two inches long. Then it rides the waves while its powerful gizzard—a section of its alimentary canal furnished with powerful muscles and tough inner walls—reduces the mussel's hard blue shell to pieces small enough to be eliminated. It must be an epic struggle.

South of New England the Atlantic flyway picks up more traffic as birds enter it from the north and northwest. The great bulk of them have nested in the Canadian prairie provinces and the flat, waterlogged country that extends all the way to the Arctic Ocean. Some of them fly down the Hudson River Valley. The smoke and glare of the giant metropolis at the terminus of the valley do not bother the birds much. They seem to know that within the built-up area around New York City they are at least safe from gunners.

Other birds, particularly those that fly down the coastline, are finding increasing security in the growing acreages of protected marsh, beach and wetland on Long Island. Set along the edges of highly developed suburban communities are eight refuges managed by the Fish and Wildlife Service. A ninth refuge, located on Long Island but within the limits of New York City, is Jamaica Bay, bounded on its eastern end by the noisy bustle of John F. Kennedy International Airport.

Except for the 26-square-mile expanse of Jamaica Bay and a 3,000-acre tract at Oyster Bay, most of these Long Island sanctuaries are small. As a result, they are off limits to casual parties of human visitors, who must—in most cases—obtain permission from the local managers to enter the refuges. Perhaps as a result, the number of migratory birds using these areas is astonishing. From mid-December through February, the 187-acre Morton National Wildlife Refuge at the eastern end of Long Island swarms with as many as 1,000 ducks at a time —primarily scaup, goldeneye and black ducks.

Migratory birds were touching down in Jamaica Bay long before New York City existed. The fact that they still do—that, in fact, they seem to be doing so in ever greater numbers—is testimony to the enormous power of a salt-marsh environment to cleanse itself. Where the bay does not abut on the airport it is almost surrounded by housing. Wastes of all kinds leach into the water, ranging from sewage to spilled jet fuel and lubricants. But the marsh fights back. Its main armor is the *Spartina* grass, which appears able to convert pollutants into plant material that can serve as pure food for birds and other marsh animals. The tides, sweeping in and out each day, bring more food from the ocean on the flood and help flush out the pollution on the ebb.

In the middle of the marsh lies the wildlife refuge managed by the New York City Department of Parks. Here two fresh-water ponds were impounded by the Parks Department in the early 1950s, providing the mixed environment of salt, brackish and fresh water that is most attractive to water birds. Around these ponds Herbert Johnson, the Parks Department supervisor who has been in charge of the refuge since 1953, has supplemented the existing bayberry and poverty grass by planting wild roses, wild cherry, chokeberries, beach plum and holly—to furnish additional food, cover and nesting material for the birds.

A glossy ibis perches on one leg in a tree at the edge of a marsh—a favored haunt where the bird's long bill enables it to probe for crayfish and worms in shallow water. Though the ibis is a tropical and subtropical species, it has begun to migrate north each year in small but growing numbers to nest and spend the summer in refuges along the New York and New Jersey coasts.

The result has been a dramatic increase in the bird population in the refuge—at least in spring and fall. In 10 years the total number of species seen and recorded in the bay climbed from a 1961 figure of 250 to more than 300. Perhaps the most exciting and significant increase has been the burgeoning of the glossy ibis, a bony marsh bird that was scarcely seen in New York state before the 1940s. Bizarre and gangling in appearance, with long legs, a downward-curving bill and dark brown iridescent plumage, the glossy ibis began to be sighted in the refuge in 1959, when five birds arrived in the bay in April and stayed until fall. By 1961, three pairs had successfully hatched offspring, the first recorded nestings in New York. Today, more than 100 pairs of ibises come to the bay each summer to make their nests, and branches of the community have spread to other parts of Long Island.

Farther south are wilder places that attract still-greater numbers of migrants. In southern New Jersey, Brigantine National Wildlife Refuge offers a particularly warm welcome. Brigantine is only 11 miles across marshes and water from Atlantic City's huddled cluster of slums and tall hotels. Established in 1939, the refuge has more than 19,500 acres, mostly salt marsh laced with shallow channels that drain at low tide to become mud flats bursting with food for water birds. Unlike Monomoy Island, which is maintained successfully in its natural state, Brigantine is carefully managed, and birds seem to love it as much as Philadelphians love Atlantic City. By the thousands, waterfowl and shore birds that seldom touch ground in New England—including Canada geese from farther west than those that fly down the coast over Cape Cod—gather at Brigantine.

The refuge is a particular haven for brant, small dark geese that nest in the extreme north and, when they migrate, fly in loose, somewhat disorganized formations. In winter brant prefer to feed on eelgrass, a land plant with ribbonlike leaves that has adapted to growing in salt water. The salt bays of the Atlantic coast used to have enormous beds of eelgrass, but in the 1930s the plant was almost killed off by a bacterial disease, and many of the brant died with it. They were rare for years, but the survivors learned to eat sea lettuce, a true algal seaweed that replaced the eelgrass. A few authorities believe that some brant might have always eaten sea lettuce and multiplied for a while, filling the ecological gap left by the eelgrass eaters.

In any case the brant made a slow recovery. But the disappearance of their eelgrass diet may have helped some stay alive that might have been shot by hunters: while eelgrass-fed brant are highly regarded by gourmets, brant that have fed on sea lettuce have a bad taste. One seaboard Virginian I talked to never got as far as tasting the dish; he told me that if you cook such a brant, you have to get out of the house, it smells so terrible. Recently the eelgrass has been coming back, and the brant have almost recovered their former numbers, but pot hunters tend to leave them alone, claiming they still taste bad.

The Fish and Wildlife Service, which operates Brigantine, has succeeded beyond its expectations in making migratory birds feel at home on the New Jersey coast. By diking large sections of marsh, the managers of the refuge impounded fresh water that mixed with the salt water—turning it brackish. This encouraged the growth of plants and small marine animals that many kinds of water birds relish. The result, at certain times of year, is an enormous gathering. During the fall migration, according to Service records, as many as 100,000 ducks and

5,000 Canada geese have crowded into Brigantine's West Pool, which covers only 896 acres.

Another experiment at Brigantine, started in 1958, was to clip the wings of six Canada geese that were on their way back to their northern nesting grounds. Having no choice, the birds settled down and raised their broods on the Brigantine marshes. The goslings grew up to consider themselves Brigantine residents. Many of their descendants continue to nest at Brigantine. Six hundred goslings were hatched there in 1970, and more than half were exported to help populate other refuges up and down the coast.

South of Brigantine are places that attract other migratory birds. Some come from overland, others from the ocean side. Most novel and interesting are the greater snow geese—white with black wing tips—that breed as far north as the northern shores of Greenland. During their journey south they always congregate for rest and food on a single large marsh on the St. Lawrence River at Cap Tourmente. From there these vigorous fliers go on to Virginia, alighting in large numbers at Chincoteague National Wildlife Refuge, part of Assateague Island. A good-sized flock of snow geese is a spectacular sight, and their arrival at their winter quarters is something to behold. Once there, the big birds seem restless, especially in windy weather, and will often make short flights apparently just for enjoyment. They take off heavily but in the air fly with deliberate, undulating grace.

Most geese have long thin necks designed for reaching down to find food under water. The necks of greater snow geese are comparatively short and muscular because their principal food is the roots and underground stems of cordgrass. Their bills are efficient cutters, which they thrust into the earth to come up with a billful of nutritious roots. Sometimes they extract the roots of cordgrass without disturbing the plant's upper parts, but usually they are less neat. At Chincoteague I saw patches of moist ground where snow geese had been feeding; the place looked as if a herd of hogs had been rooting for peanuts.

The most spectacular bird of all, the whistling swan, joins the flyway in Virginia, having flown all the way from its nesting grounds in northern Alaska and northwestern Canada. These pure-white birds, with a wingspread over four feet, fly in perfect "V"s, with slow wing beats but at great speed, up to 60 miles per hour. Like snow geese, they seem to enjoy putting on exhibitions of grace in flight. I don't know why they are called whistling swans—perhaps for the sound of their wings. Actually, their cry is a conversational honk, not quite as musical as that of the Canada geese. When feeding at night whistling swans can be extremely noisy, their voices carrying for miles.

A favorite wintering ground for whistling swans, as well as for snow geese, Canada geese and numerous kinds of ducks, is Back Bay National Wildlife Refuge in the southeast corner of Virginia, fronting the Atlantic about 25 miles south of the mouth of Chesapeake Bay. On a visit in December I was shown around Back Bay by a very agreeable man named Romie Waterfield.

We saw lots of muskrats, and he explained how they improve the duck forage by opening up the matted marsh grass so the ducks can get down and find the seeds and tender shoots and flush out the small insects and crustaceans they prefer to eat.

The birds eventually get such a feel for their sanctuary that they come to know its limits. During the open hunting season they stay carefully inside the boundary, which is marked by conspicuous signs, while hunters prowl outside. "Ducks can't read," Mr. Waterfield told me, "but some of the hunters think they can. So they sneak in here after dark and put gunny sacks over the signs. It doesn't do any good. The birds still know what the signs mean."

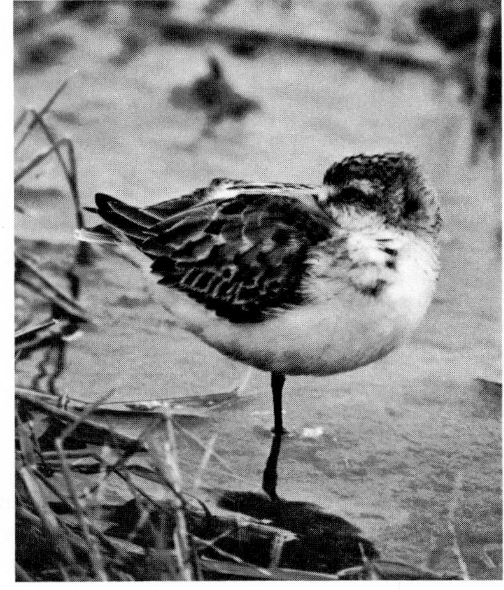

Balancing on one leg, its bill tucked under its wing, a sandpiper, one of 57 species of North American shore birds, takes its ease among the reeds in the shallows of a Cape Hatteras salt marsh.

Back Bay swarms with birds, but the most conspicuous by far are the whistling swans that sit on the water in gleaming white thousands, often organized in cozy family groups—whistling swans mate for life. "Along about the middle of March," said Mr. Waterfield, "I can tell they've got something on their minds. They're all on pins and needles, fidgety. They fly a little way and settle down. They talk to each other; sometimes they all holler at once. They squall all night, a different call. Then early one morning I see the time has come. They take off in flocks of from 30 up to 100. I see them organize into their 'V's. They point northwest for Alaska. In three days all are gone, and that's the last we see of them until the next fall."

Not all is happy in Mr. Waterfield's fortunate kingdom. It is only 30 miles from the center of Virginia Beach, a community with a population of 188,000—an increase of 1,000 per cent since 1960. A four-mile-wide stretch of open beach along Back Bay's shoreline is legally open to vehicles. In warm weather swarms of beach buggies roar along it. "We counted two hundred per hour last summer," Mr. Waterfield told me, "and the traffic is doubling every year."

I asked him to show me that beach, and it was a sad sight. The littered sand was deeply rutted down to the edge of the water. The dune was eroding fast. We saw no shore birds at all and only one sea gull.

"This beach was fine," said Mr. Waterfield, "before the buggies came. It was like the way Assateague is now. The sand was full of ghost crabs. The terns nested on it, and we had lots of shore birds. Loggerhead turtles, some of them weighing half a ton, hauled out to lay their eggs. Now there's nothing but buggies and beer cans and garbage. The ghost crabs are gone. They got squashed. So are the shore birds. The traffic running on the wet sand crushes the little things they live on. Some of the loggerheads try to come ashore but are scared away by the traffic. We helped a few of them across the beach to lay their eggs, but it didn't do any good. When the little turtles hatched, they couldn't climb out of the ruts. So they got crushed too."

Mr. Waterfield is not cheerful about the beach-buggy problem, but he points to the next beach to the north, which belongs to the city of Virginia Beach. It is barred to vehicles and is wide, clean and rutless.

Far from centers of population, Pea Island National Wildlife Refuge, a 13-mile section of Hatteras Island on North Carolina's Outer Banks, is one of the birds' favorite stopping places. Its area is only 6,700 acres—the narrow island is hardly more than a beach, dunes and a strip of marsh—but within this area the birds are secure against hunters. They are, indeed, almost arrogant. Canada geese, greater snow geese and whistling swans feed unconcernedly near the highway, paying no attention to passing cars. Even when a car stops and people get out of it, the geese do not always fly away. Once I pointed a stick at some of them, but they knew I was fooling. They looked at me for a while and went back to feeding. The whistling swans are highly visible here, sweeping across the road just above the power line in their beautiful "V"s, talking to each other. In places where they are not protected they are extremely wary and are seldom seen except high in the air or as specks of white bobbing far out on a bay.

As one of the more southerly refuges, Pea Island is comparatively warm, and the waterfowl know this well. Whenever a cold spell freezes the feeding grounds in more northerly refuges, the birds swarm down to Pea Island like New Yorkers fleeing to Miami ahead of a January blizzard. As a result, the island provides a haven for almost every species of duck that uses the flyway, except for the eiders, which enjoy cold weather and open water.

The number of national wildlife refuges along the continental Atlantic flyway is increasing steadily: as the 1970s began, there were 71, compared to 50 in 1960. The birds have more places to spend the winter, to rest on their arduous journeys north to breed, and to feel safe from hunters all the year round. The more refuges there are, the more birds there will be to travel the flyway. But human population along the Atlantic seaboard is also increasing, and so are automobiles, which cause more noise and mess than their owners. Because of this, wildlife authorities know that there will never again be flocks of birds in numbers enough to darken the sky. But the managers of the wildlife refuges are cheered by a rather recent development: some of the wild birds are learning to take advantage of man without losing the wildness that is their great charm. For one thing, most of them know exactly where the sanctuaries are. Furthermore, annoyed hunters have told me that the birds can tell time accurately. As soon as a legal shooting period ends they fly everywhere with abandon.

In the early years the wooded uplands adjoining the flyway offered little or no food for most kinds of water birds, and after they became cultivated fields the birds still avoided them. Now, I am told, the Canada geese, one of the most adaptable water birds, have learned that the green leaves of young wheat are excellent forage in fall. Cornfields were not much attraction as long as the ears were hand-gathered in the husk, but the mechanical picker that has come into almost universal use chews up the ears and scatters ample corn for the birds to glean. Snow geese and various kinds of ducks have taken to following the Canada geese to these rich new feeding grounds. Conservationists hope they will also learn how to glean peanut and soybean fields. If this happens, some of the most attractive water birds may have a population explosion like that of the omnivorous herring gulls when they learned to take advantage of man's refuse heaps.

Land's End

PHOTOGRAPHS BY PAUL CAPONIGRO

To photographer Paul Caponigro, beaches "have always conveyed a sense of mystery and primitive power." Seeking to renew and expand these impressions, Caponigro set out to photograph a northern beach in the dead of winter, when the harsh weather and the bleak gray light were certain to intensify the starkness of the scene.

The site he chose was remote Montauk Point, whose 20 miles of beach rim the eastern end of Long Island in New York. The pictures shown here are the result of his four days' work in the blustery cold of mid-December. From time to time, when the wind died down and the sun broke through the overcast, the sea displayed a calm, gleaming, almost summery face. But there were few such moments.

The desolation at Montauk confirmed Caponigro's sense of elemental forces at work. Hundreds of broken sea shells, mingled with seaweed, littered one stretch of beach. On another beach Caponigro found the skeleton of a large fish, stripped clean by waves and scavengers. More dramatic were the signs of the sea's brute strength. Strong breakers, generated by many winter gales, had destroyed a section of bluff and left a group of boulders strangely isolated in the middle of one beach. At the back of another, undermining waves had sheered off the face of a bluff, exposing the roots of grasses in a ragged fringe.

While savoring the sea's raw energy at the water's edge, Caponigro also probed inland to find a contrasting theme. He discovered it in a peaceful field of tall marsh reeds, their stalks as delicate and finely etched as a Japanese print. Back on the beach, Caponigro found that the sea in a tranquil mood could also create exquisite effects. He was particularly fascinated by the thin swash marks of marine debris left behind on the beach by a gentle ebb tide; he later described these long fragile traceries as "a visual echo of the sound of the surf."

For Caponigro, the mysterious essence of the beach seemed most palpable when fog shrouded the shore. "The effect was hallucinatory," he recalled. "The ocean and the shore and the sky seemed to overlap and then intermingle. I grew more and more conscious of the constant pounding of the surf and the penetrating odor of sea salt. Finally, the land disappeared entirely, and I felt as if the sea were all around me."

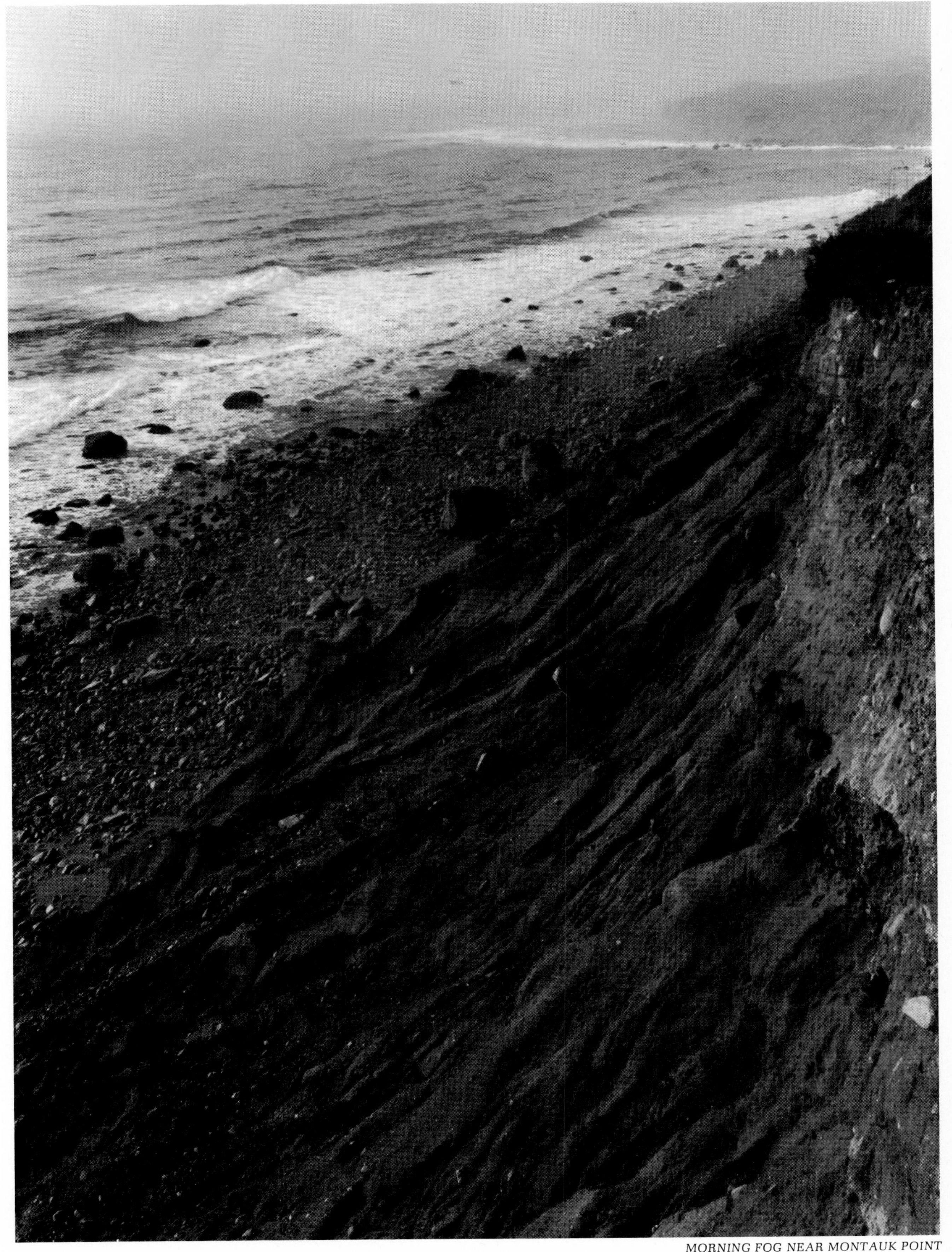

MORNING FOG NEAR MONTAUK POINT

A BLUFF UNDERCUT BY WAVES

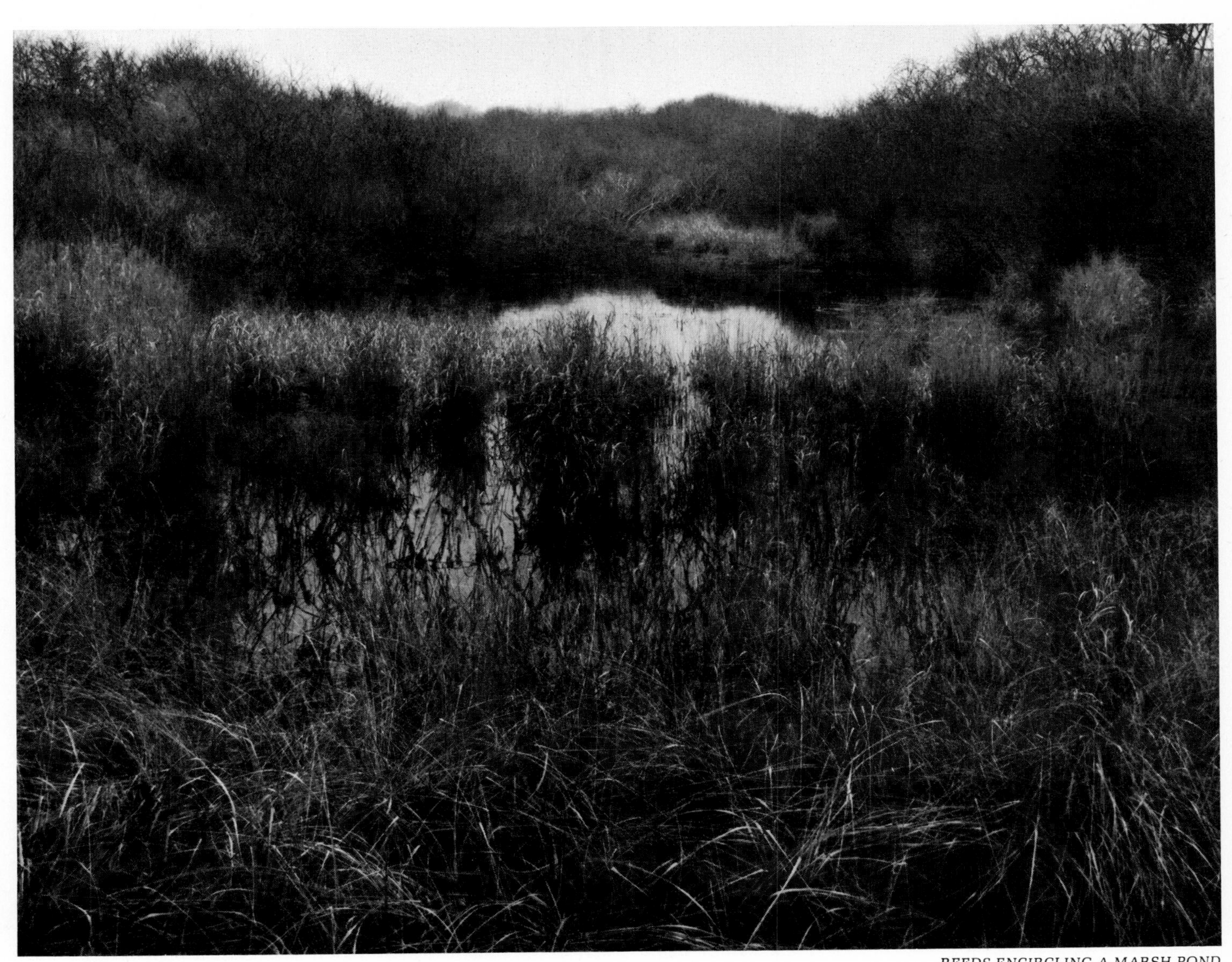

REEDS ENCIRCLING A MARSH POND

WHITE WATER ALONG THE SOUTH SHORE

CONCENTRIC SWASH MARKS ON THE SAND

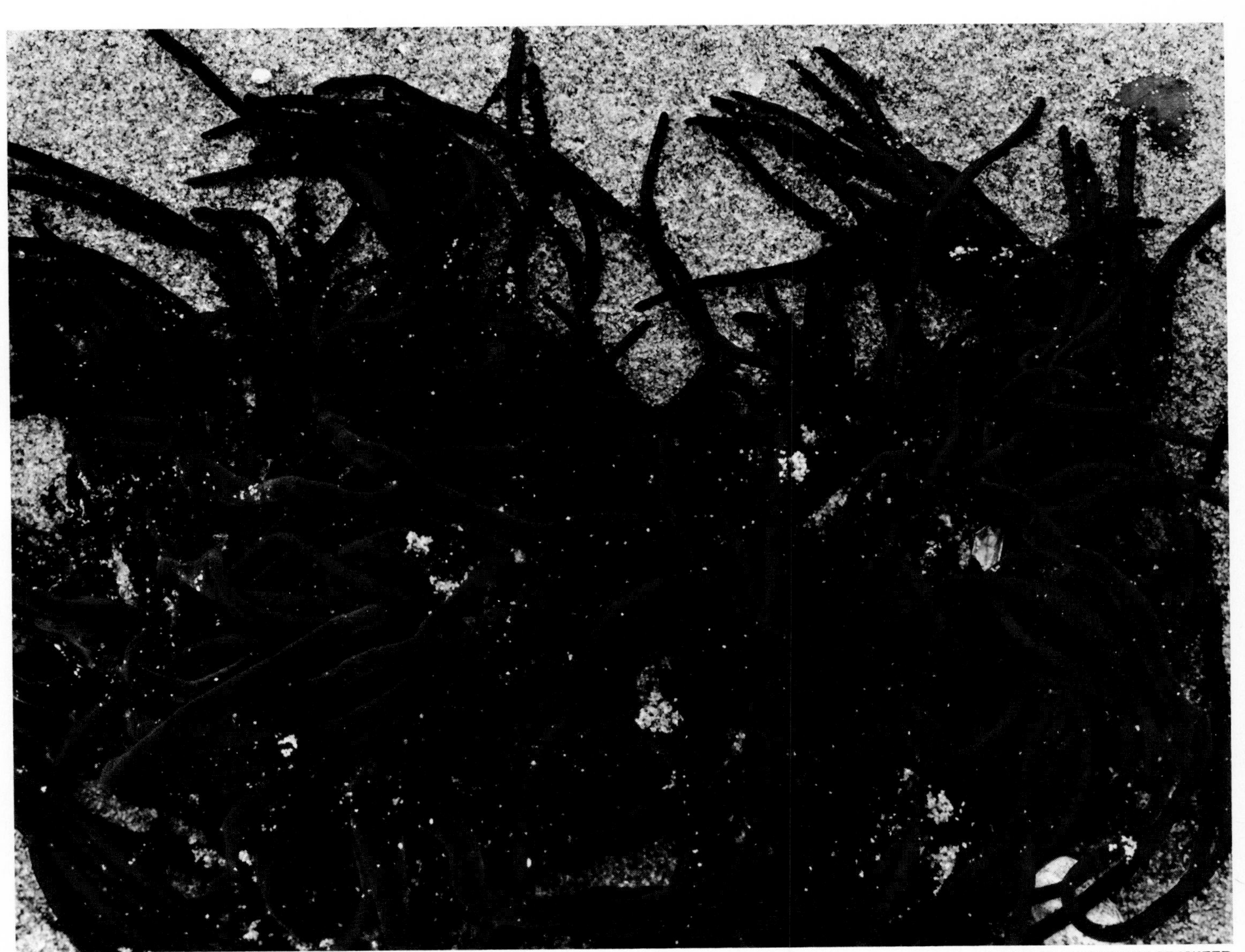

A CLUMP OF CODIUM SEAWEED

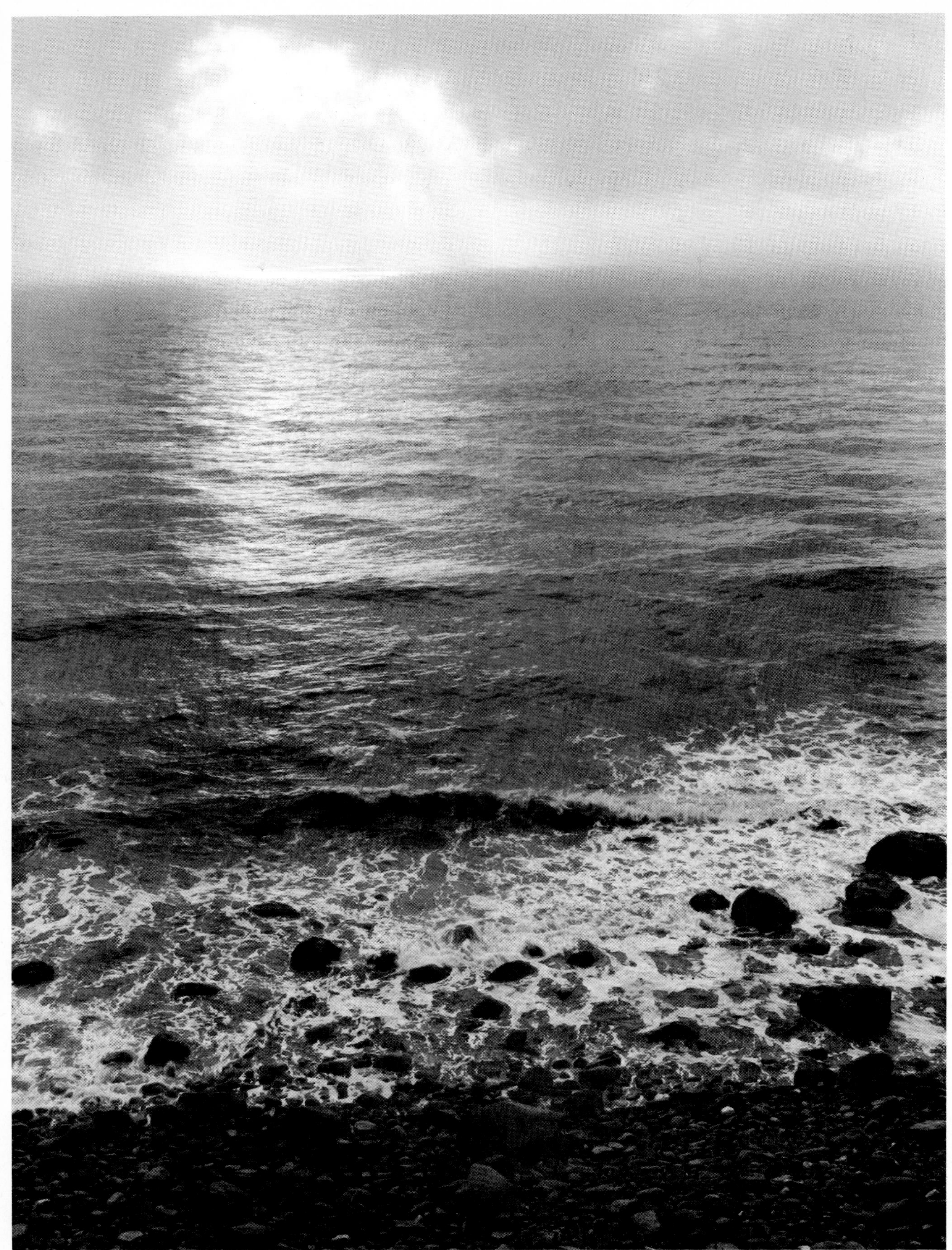

SUN GLEAMING THROUGH A WINTER MIST

BOULDERS LEFT BEHIND IN THE SHORELINE'S RETREAT

STONES AND A FISH SKELETON FRAMED BY AN ERODING MORAINE

Bibliography

**Also available in paperback.*
†Available in paperback only.

Amos, William H., *The Life of the Seashore*. McGraw-Hill, 1966.

†Bascom, Willard, *Waves and Beaches*. Anchor Books, Doubleday & Company, 1964.

Berrill, N. J. and Jacquelyn, *1001 Questions Answered about the Seashore*. Dodd, Mead & Company, 1959.

†Beston, Henry, *The Outermost House*. The Viking Press, 1961.

*Carson, Rachel, *The Edge of the Sea*. Signet Books, 1955.

Chamberlain, Barbara, *These Fragile Outposts*. Natural History Press, 1964.

†Chapman, Frank, *Handbook of Birds of Eastern North America*. Dover Publications, 1966.

Hall, Henry Marion, *A Gathering of Shore Birds*. The Devin-Adair Company, 1960.

*Hay, John, and Peter Farb, *The Atlantic Shore*. Harper & Row, 1969.

Hay, John, *The Sandy Shore*. The Chatham Press, 1968.

Kittredge, Henry C., *Cape Cod, Its People and Their History*. Houghton Mifflin Company, 1968.

Kortright, Francis, *The Ducks, Geese and Swans of North America*. The Stackpole Company, 1953.

Miner, Roy W., *Field Book of Seashore Life*. G. P. Putnam's Sons, 1950.

Ogburn, Charlton, Jr., *The Winter Beach*. William Morrow & Company, 1966.

†Petry, Loren C., *A Beachcomber's Botany*. The Chatham Conservation Foundation, 1968.

Ray, Carleton, and Elgin Ciampi, *The Underwater Guide to Marine Life*. A. S. Barnes and Company, 1956.

Richardson, Wyman, *The House on Nauset Marsh*. W. W. Norton & Company, 1955.

Snyder, Leslie L., *Arctic Birds of Canada*. University of Toronto Press, 1957.

Sterling, Dorothy, *The Outer Lands*. The Natural History Press, 1967.

Stick, David, *The Outer Banks of North Carolina*. The University of North Carolina Press, 1958.

Stout, Gardner D., ed., *The Shorebirds of North America*. The Viking Press, 1968.

†Strahler, Arthur N., *A Geologist's View of Cape Cod*. The Natural History Press, 1966.

*Teal, John and Mildred, *Life and Death of the Salt Marsh*. Little, Brown and Company, 1970.

*Thoreau, Henry D., *Cape Cod*. Thomas Crowell Company, 1961.

†Truitt, Reginald V., *Assateague . . the "Place Across."* Natural Resources Institute, University of Maryland, 1971.

Williams, Russ, *The Ways of Wildfowl*. J. G. Ferguson, 1971.

Acknowledgments

The author and editors of this book wish to thank the following: J. C. Appel, Manager, Chincoteague National Wildlife Refuge, Chincoteague, Virginia; B. E. Barrett, Department of Natural Sciences, Roger Williams College, Bristol, Rhode Island; Donald Bruning, Assistant Curator of Birds, New York Zoological Society, The Zoological Park, Bronx; Bob Burgoon, Assistant Manager, Brigantine National Wildlife Refuge, Oceanville, New Jersey; Michael Castagna, Scientist-in-Charge, Virginia Institute of Marine Science, Eastern Shore Laboratory, Wachapreague, Virginia; Walter Crissey, Director, Bureau of Sport Fisheries and Wildlife Migratory Bird Population Station, Laurel, Maryland; Patrick D. Crosland, Naturalist, Fire Island National Seashore, Patchogue, New York; Robert Dolan, Professor of Environmental Sciences, The University of Virginia, Charlottesville; William Drury, Director of Research, The Massachusetts Audubon Society, Lincoln; George E. Gage, Manager, Long Island National Wildlife Refuges, Huntington, New York; H. J. Grove, Interpretive Specialist, Division of Wildlife Refuges, Bureau of Sport Fisheries and Wildlife, U.S. Department of the Interior, Washington, D.C.; Dennis F. Holland, Manager, Back Bay National Wildlife Refuge, Virginia Beach, Virginia; Sidney Horenstein, Department of Invertebrate Paleontology, The American Museum of Natural History, New York City; Larry K. Malone, Manager, Monomoy National Wildlife Refuge, Concord, Massachusetts; Vince Mrazek, Chief Naturalist, Cape Hatteras National Seashore, Manteo, North Carolina; The Nature Conservancy, Arlington, Virginia; Larry Pardue, The New York Botanical Garden, Bronx; Alfred C. Redfield, Woods Hole Oceanographic Institution, Woods Hole, Massachusetts; Preston D. Riddel, Assistant Superintendent, Cape Hatteras National Seashore, Manteo, North Carolina; John Teal, Senior Scientist, Woods Hole Oceanographic Institution, Woods Hole, Massachusetts; Marvin Wass, Virginia Institute of Marine Science, Eastern Shore Laboratory, Wachapreague, Virginia; Romie Waterfield, Biological Technician, Back Bay National Wildlife Refuge, Virginia Beach, Virginia; N. F. Williamson, Manager, Pea Island National Wildlife Refuge, Manteo, North Carolina; John Wise, Interpretive Specialist, Assateague National Seashore, Berlin, Maryland.

Picture Credits

The sources for the pictures in this book are shown below. Credits for the pictures from left to right are separated by commas.

Cover–Harald Sund. Front end papers 2, 3–Harald Sund. Front end paper 4, page 1–Robert Walch. 2, 3–Harald Sund. 4, 5–Costa Manos from Magnum. 6, 7–Thomas E. Mahnken Jr. 8, 9–Dean Brown. 14, 15–Map by R. R. Donnelley Cartographic Services. 20, 21–David Robinson. 25–Harald Sund. 31 through 41–Harald Sund. 44–Thoreau Society, Inc. 49–Peabody Museum of Salem photo by M. W. Sexton. 54, 55–Harald Sund. 61 through 69–Robert Walch. 72 –Thomas E. Mahnken Jr. 74, 75–William D. Griffin. 78, 79–W. M. Stephens. 82, 83, 84–Harald Sund. 91 through 97 –Harald Sund. 102, 103–Costa Manos from Magnum. 104–Fred Ward from Black Star. 110, 111–National Park Service photo by M. Woodbridge Williams. 118, 119–Costa Manos from Magnum. 120–Jack Dermid. 123–Henry Groskinsky for LIFE. 127, 128, 129–Costa Manos from Magnum. 130, 131 –Costa Manos from Magnum except center bottom Jack Dermid. 132, 133 –Costa Manos from Magnum. 138, 139 –Jack Dermid. 143–Zigmund Leszczynski from ANIMALS ANIMALS. 144 –NASA. 149–Bruce Roberts from Rapho-Guillumette. 150, 151–National Park Service photo by M. Woodbridge Williams. 152, 153–Tom Sennett, William D. Griffin. 154–Thomas W. Martin from Rapho-Guillumette. 155, 156, 157 –William D. Griffin. 162–A. W. Ambler from The National Audubon Society. 165–Dean Brown. 169 through 179–Paul Caponigro.

Index

Numerals in italics indicate a photograph or drawing of the subject mentioned.

Printed in U.S.A.

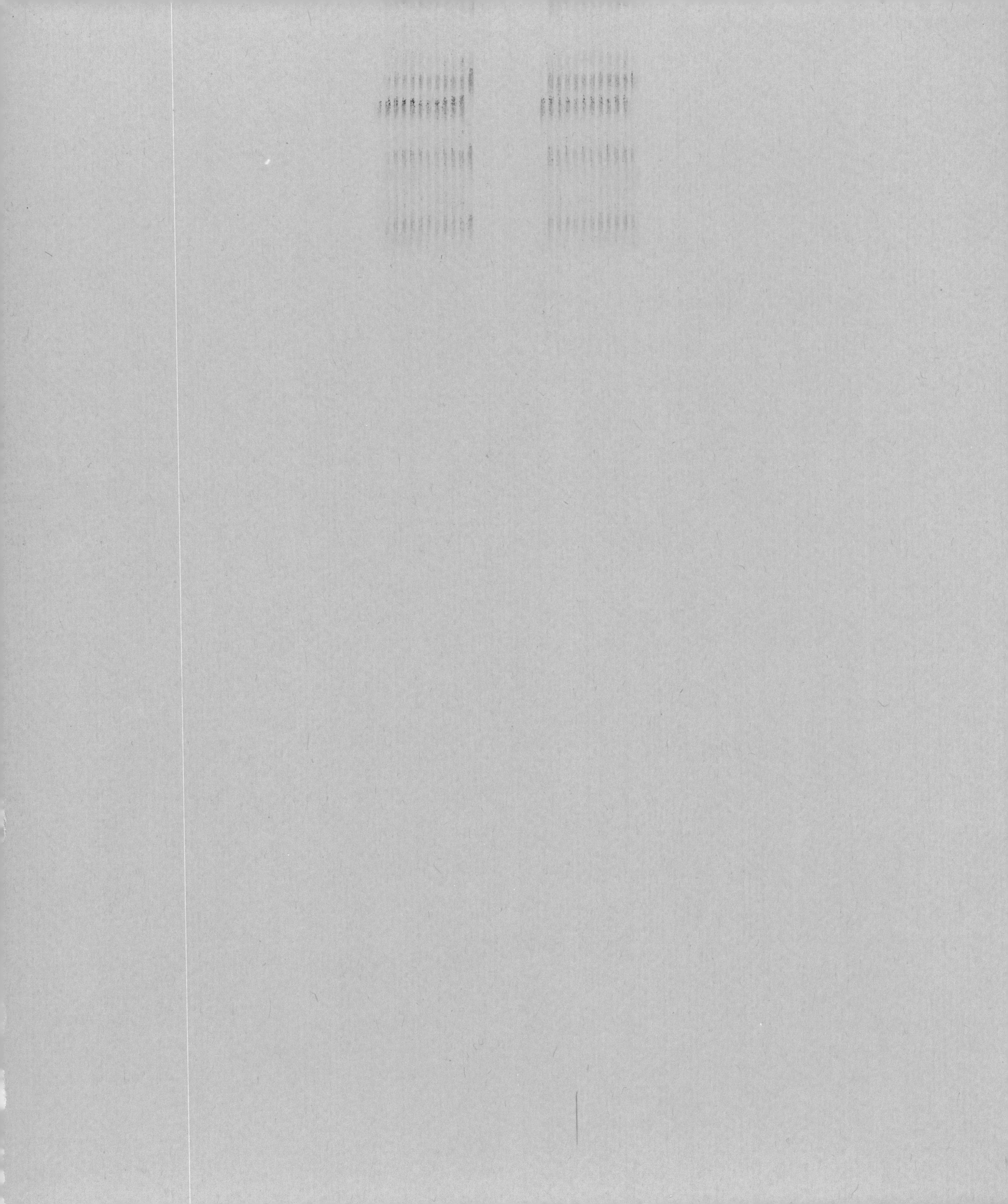